ONLY SAY GOOD THINGS

ONLY SAY GOOD THINGS

Surviving *Playboy* and Finding Myself

CRYSTAL HEFNER

GRAND
CENTRAL

NEW YORK   BOSTON

Jacket design by Albert Tang
Jacket photograph by Peter Yang
Jacket © 2024 Hachette Book Group, Inc.

Grand Central Publishing
Hachette Book Group
1290 Avenue of the Americas, New York, NY 10104
grandcentralpublishing.com
twitter.com/grandcentralpub

First Edition: January 2024

Grand Central Publishing is a division of Hachette Book Group, Inc. The Grand Central Publishing name and logo is a trademark of Hachette Book Group, Inc.

The publisher is not responsible for websites (or their content) that are not owned by the publisher.

The Hachette Speakers Bureau provides a wide range of authors for speaking events. To find out more, go to hachettespeakersbureau.com or email HachetteSpeakers@hbgusa.com.

Grand Central Publishing books may be purchased in bulk for business, educational, or promotional use. For information, please contact your local bookseller or the Hachette Book Group Special Markets Department at special.markets@hbgusa.com.

Library of Congress Control Number: 2023945939

ISBNs: 978-1-5387-6567-8 (Hardcover); 978-1-5387-6569-2 (ebook)

Printed in the United States of America

LSC-C

Printing 1, 2023

For anyone who has ever felt lost on their journey to self-love and self-acceptance—you are not alone.

CONTENTS

CONTENTS

The Promise

Last night I dreamed about the mansion again.

In the dream I am driving, racing to get back before curfew. The sun is already setting, the L.A. light turning golden in my rearview mirror. I'm panicking because while I don't know what will happen if I arrive past my curfew, I know I can't be late, and the terror claws and scrapes at my throat. I press on the gas pedal, desperately trying to go faster, to make it back to that ivy-covered Gothic house surrounded by redwoods before the clock strikes six. But in the way of dreams, everything is in slow motion, everything is strange and unfamiliar, and the road stretches on and on. In my dream I know I'm not going to make it in time. I know that this road will never get me to where I need to be.

I know that I am lost.

I wake up with old familiar feelings: sick, anxious, afraid.

It's been years since I lived in the mansion. I haven't been back since my husband died. He died, I left, and I never went back. But I seem to go back there in my mind all the time. Much more than I want to. And not just when I'm dreaming.

1

In a lot of ways, I am still trying to get out of that mansion.

I always had to be home by six o'clock. If I wasn't, it was a problem. He would be upset. He would be yelling my name through the house. The pantry staff would start frantically calling my phone at exactly 6:01 p.m., even though I'd already be winding my way up the long, curving drive, around the tall stone fountain topped with a cherub watching me with its empty marble eyes. And then I would run in, pushing through the heavy wooden door, and go find Hef, so I could kiss him on the cheek and show him: Here I am, I'm home, I've followed the rules.

I'm a good girl.

For almost a decade, the Playboy Mansion was my home. But it never really felt like home. It felt like a place I was forever visiting. Like a hotel I'd checked into, but could never leave. Like a stage I was performing on, observed by so many sets of faceless eyes. Sometimes it felt like going back in time—Hef had decorated the house to the nines back in the seventies, and everything looked exactly the same as it had then: the deep shag carpets, the wood paneling and chandeliers, the heavy velvet drapes. I was never allowed to change a thing.

There was only one place I ever managed to make my own: a tiny room we called the vanity, just a closet really, but with a handful of long, narrow windows. The vanity was right off the primary bedroom, or master bedroom as it was called by Hef. It had a flimsy door that slid shut but didn't lock. There was just enough space for a small, built-in desk and chair. It was my little sanctuary, a place to be alone and unobserved. In the mansion, there was always someone in every room—other girls, party guests, staff. There was a friend of Hef's on the couch next to me, leaning uncomfortably close. There was a famous movie star in the hallway who wanted to run his hands over me. There were no doors I could lock because there were copies of every key. And Hef, of course, held the master key that ensured no one could ever lock him out. This was his world, and he held the key to everyone and everything.

In the vanity, for a few minutes at least, I could lay my head down on my arms and stop the pretense. Stop worrying about what I looked like every second.

Whether I was smiling the right way.

Whether I had arranged my body correctly.

Whether I was dressed the way he liked.

Whether my hair looked right.

Whether my breasts were perfect enough.

How I compared to the other women. There were always other women around. It was always, explicitly, a competition.

I used to steal brief moments in the vanity—small shining moments when I could breathe deeply and not have to be "on." Playing the role of someone else's image of you every day and every night is exhausting—physically, mentally, and in a way that feels like your soul is actually tired, like some kind of life energy battery is running low.

The vanity's second-story window opened out onto the lawn, where peacocks strolled and staff crisscrossed carrying chairs and platters of food and cases of wine, getting ready for this party or that one. Ivy grew around that window, thick on the stone, like in a fairy tale. Sometimes I imagined myself as Rapunzel, locked in her tower, waiting for someone to rescue her. But nobody ever did. And I had climbed into my tower voluntarily.

I didn't know then that I could rescue myself. I didn't always know I needed to be rescued, but I knew I was trapped.

The peacocks on the lawn were beautiful but territorial, especially when they were mating. At times the noises they made sounded like cats dying, but at other times they sounded like women screaming, their cries echoing through my small closet until even with the window shut I could hear their plaintive voices in my mind. "Help, help," they cawed and wailed; at least that's what it sounded like to me.

I sometimes think about all the women who sat at that desk—all of us believing this small, contained space represented something so much bigger. Success. Glamour. Freedom. Holly even had her initials carved into the ornate wood—until, years into my marriage, I had them sanded away. I didn't replace them with my own initials. The desk was a permanent fixture in a house where I was not. It was where I lived, but it was never my home. There was very little in that huge, opulent house that belonged to me.

I spent a decade of my life at the Playboy Mansion. First, I was just a guest—a dazzled, starry-eyed girl at a party. Then, I became a girlfriend. I became a member of arguably the most high-profile, visible modern harem in existence. I became a *Playboy* centerfold—that holy grail of success in the *Playboy* world—on newsstands across the country. I became the fiancée of one of the most powerful, controversial, mythical men in the public imagination. And then I left, and became his "runaway bride"—the only one he ever chased after. Eventually, I became his wife. At the end, I became his caretaker. And when he died, I became a widow—and a symbol. Officially, first as vice president and then as president of the board at the Hugh Hefner Foundation, it was my job to help keep the foundation well funded and well regarded. Unofficially, it was also my job to embody the *Playboy* myth, to embody the Hugh Hefner myth. He had worked so hard for more than seven decades to control the narrative of who he was and how he was, and in his mind, perpetuating this story was the most valuable thing he left me when he died.

I've only ever told a small slice of my story. I've only ever told the shiny, glamorous parts—the parts that people wanted to hear. The good pieces. Partly, this was because I didn't want to see myself as a victim. Partly, this was because I didn't want to upset his family. Mostly, this was because I'd made a promise to Hef.

My last year at the mansion, Hef wanted me near him at all times. I had always had a curfew, but now it was bumped earlier and earlier. When he didn't know where I was, he whipped up the staff into a frenzy to find me. He was frail and tired, but he rarely talked about death. The only thing he wanted to make sure I knew was that he wanted to be buried in Westwood Village Memorial Park next to Marilyn Monroe. He had already bought the crypt for seventy-five thousand dollars back in the nineties. He said he didn't care about the funeral service; he would leave all those details to me.

"I won't be there," was all he said. "Do whatever you want."

All he cared about was that he ended up in the slot he'd bought, right next to Marilyn's. She was the first woman to grace the cover of *Playboy* and to appear nude inside its pages. He put her in there without her permission, after buying the photos from a calendar company. She never got a dime. And she certainly didn't have any say in whose bones would be lying next to hers for all eternity.

I didn't say a word. If that's what he wanted, that's what he would get. Hef always got what he wanted.

He told me a lot that he loved me.

He told me he'd be waiting for me on the other side. I tried to see this as a nice thing, but it felt oppressive, almost like a threat.

I used to go out for drives during the day, just to get out of that house. Every time I drove away I thought about the time I was prevented from leaving. The time I had to sneak past security guards in order to escape. And the time I willingly went back.

I would drive around L.A., a city I didn't know well, because for ten years I'd been sealed up inside that house. Once, I drove all the way to San Diego, through the gritty neighborhoods where I grew up, moving around from apartment to apartment after my dad died; past the swankier neighborhoods where we lived when my mom was dating someone who had money.

I'd drive past the campus of the college I'd once gone to, majoring in psychology and dreaming of helping others. I drove past the tiny apartment I once lived in. I drove past the cemetery where my first love was buried, years ago, when we were both so young. I drove to the beach where my dad used to love to fish—the ocean was always his favorite place to be. I drove through all the loss and grief and confusion and mistakes I had made, and wondered who I would be if I hadn't been bused to the Playboy Mansion for a Halloween party one long-ago night. I was responsible for my choices, but the cost felt so much higher than I could have ever imagined at the age of twenty-one.

I called my mom sometimes on these drives—she was one of the only people I could really confide in. At the mansion, I didn't have any real friends. Anyone and everyone would stab you in the back given half a chance. Everyone was a spy. My mom and I have had our ups and downs, but I could always tell her anything. I would vent to her about how trapped I felt, how panicky, how sometimes it felt hard to breathe, like there was an iron band around my chest, keeping me from ever taking a deep enough breath.

"Honey," she said to me, so many times, "you have money saved. You don't have to stay there. Just pack up your stuff and go!"

"I can't leave him," I'd tell her. And then I'd drive faster because I was worried I had been gone too long. And because I knew I had left once, and I ended up just as lost.

Once upon a time I had desperately needed Hugh Hefner, and then, later, he desperately needed me.

Hef's ninety-first birthday, in April of 2017, was his last. It was exactly the same as every birthday that had come before it. The theme, as always, was *Casablanca*. He loved old movies—the black-and-white classics, where the women were damsels in distress and the men were manly and strong—but *Casablanca* was his all-time favorite. We screened it on his birthday every year, in the movie room, with all the party guests in costume: the men in white tuxedos, the women in slinky 1930s dresses. The dining room was tricked out like Rick's Cafe, with posters on the walls and decorations that hinted at a dusty Moroccan expat bar. At the end of the movie, when Rick and Ilsa parted ways, he cried. Something about the doomed romance really got to him. By now I knew that he could be very sentimental.

He could also be very cruel.

That night, on his ninety-first birthday, he cried at the end of the movie as he always did. He turned to look at me with tears in his eyes, showing me that he was upset, as if to say, *Do something! I'm sad!*

I took his hand, gave him a kiss.

He used to dress up as Bogie, in a full white tuxedo, but now he didn't have the energy for it anymore. Instead, he wore his usual silk pajamas—black this time—and I draped a white tuxedo jacket over his shoulders, an attempt to replicate earlier parties. After the movie, everyone streamed into the dining room. I held Hef's arm, and he leaned on me—hard. It was difficult for him to walk, but I didn't want anybody to see that. He still had to be Hugh Hefner for all these people. He couldn't be an old man. Like the women he adorned himself with, he couldn't show anything as unpalatable as natural aging. In the movies he watched over and over again, the actors never changed. They didn't age, they didn't evolve, they didn't make different life choices.

Hef was ninety-one, but in his mind it was always forty years ago—his hair was thick and dark, his pipe was lit, and women were always grateful, willing, and eager. Even as he leaned on me to walk on his birthday, in his mind he was still the man all other men wanted to be and all women wanted to fuck. The one with all the power and control.

There were platters of lobster and thousand-dollar tins of caviar laid out on the table. The staff poured champagne into coupe glasses until they overflowed. The typical excess of the Playboy world. I stood holding his arm, letting him lean on me without letting on. Flashes went off as people took photos. People were always taking photos. In the mansion, you had to think about how you might look splashed on the pages of a magazine at all times. You had to always be conscious of your face, your body; how you were holding yourself and what expression you were making. Right now I was trying to look the part of the happy wife.

When they brought the cake out, it was perfectly airbrushed, the same as always: his face and mine screened onto the icing. Hef as Bogart, me his blond Bergman. Before me, it had been Holly's face on the cake; before that Tina, Brande, Kimberly . . . a parade of blondes, each one of us replacing the last.

"Blow out the candles!" I said. I smiled and clapped.

In the photos from that night, I am laughing. My makeup is flawless, and my dress sparkles. My golden blond hair has been done in big sexy waves, classic *Playboy* style. What the cameras don't capture is everything I'm hiding: that he's dying, that I'm also sick. That I can feel in my body that something is very wrong. I'm exhausted. My brain is foggy; I can barely think. It feels like my bones are burning. I've been to see doctor after doctor, trying to figure out what's wrong; I've been on an intensive course of antibiotics; I've had surgery to remove the breast implants I had put in over a decade ago. I still feel horrible. Shaky. Weak. I don't know what's wrong, but something is telling me: *This mansion is killing me.*

I am only thirty-one, but like Hef, I feel like I am old, like I am also dying.

At the end of the night, Hef's two burly ex-military nurses carried him up the stairs. I helped him change out of the black silk pajamas and into the flannel ones he now preferred to sleep in. I helped him into the bed. The bed was huge, elaborately carved. The mirror still hung on the ceiling, the one he used to like to look up at when he was lying on this bed surrounded by women at his disposal. That night, like so many nights, he wanted to talk about his legacy, and how the Hugh Hefner name would carry on after he died. He always said he wanted to be remembered as someone who made an impression. Someone who changed the sexual mores of his time. He wanted to be a giant of American history: respected, admired, and heroic.

"I want you to be on the board of my foundation," he was saying as I slipped his slippers off and lifted his pale, almost translucent, legs under the silk sheets. "I want you to continue my legacy going forward."

And then he paused and looked at me.

"And I want to remind you," he said, his eyes locked on mine, "to only say good things about me."

He had a way of being imperious and condescending even when he was asking for a favor.

I hesitated, but barely.

"Of course," I said.

"Promise me," he replied.

I looked at him, so frail and weak and small in this big bed, and I swallowed down every part of me that wanted to say so much more. "I will only say good things, I promise."

He smiled then, and patted the empty space in the bed next to him. He was asleep before I even got into bed, but I lay awake for a long time after, thinking about my promise. It felt exactly like what it was: a heavy weight that I was supposed to carry forever.

Six months later, he came down with a minor infection. At first, it seemed treatable—the doctors just had to identify the correct antibiotic to treat this particular strain of bacteria, and he would be fine. Sure, he was in his nineties, but he'd made it through much worse. He'd made it through cancer. But it was an E. coli infection—an aggressive one. When the doctors started suggesting he wasn't going to make it, I was confused and frantic. I'd desperately wanted out of the mansion, the marriage, but not like this. Death has always been a trigger for me—whether death of people or animals. When something is about to die I am instantly a child in panic and fear, desperate to stop it from coming into the house. I started calling doctors I knew in L.A. who might have other antibiotics in stock. If I found the right one, I just knew I could save him.

But I couldn't.

After he died, the media hounded me for a statement. My phone buzzed and buzzed with requests from every news outlet imaginable. At the gates, a pile of bouquets grew higher and higher. Periodically, so that people could go in and out, staff had to go down and clear them away, armloads of crumpled cellophane and dying flowers. There were cards and letters, all about how much he meant to people. He would have loved the outpouring; he would have captured each note and created another scrapbook of the adulation. He had thousands of scrapbooks, arranged by topic, by events and times he wanted to remember.

I didn't leave at all in those first few weeks. I stayed inside. I didn't know what to do, where to go. Even more deeply, I didn't know what I wanted to do or even who I was outside of those gates.

But I was going to have to figure it out—and fast.

The mansion had already been sold, more than a year prior, to a billionaire who wanted to own a piece of *Playboy*. The agreement with the new owner was that he would allow Hef to continue living in the mansion, undisturbed, for the rest of his life. Now he was gone, and the mansion didn't belong to any of us anymore. We had to get out.

Finally, I sat down, wrote a statement, and sent it to the publicist at *Playboy*. She made edits and then we sent it out to the world.

"I haven't been able to bring myself to write most people back to thank them for their condolences," I wrote. "I am heartbroken. I am still in disbelief. We laid him to rest Saturday. He is in the place he was always certain he wanted to spend eternity. He was an American hero. A pioneer. A kind and humble soul who opened up his life and home to the world. I felt how much he loved me. I loved him so much. I am so grateful. He gave me life. He gave me direction. He taught me kindness. I will feel eternally grateful to have been by his side, holding his hand, and telling him how much I loved him. He changed my life, he saved my life. He made me feel loved every single day. He was a beacon to the world, a force unlike anything else. There has never been and never will be another Hugh M. Hefner."

I only said good things.

When I wrote that statement, I meant it. I was heartbroken. I was shattered. I was in shock that he was gone. He seemed eternal in so many ways, even as he faded over those last years—like something that would go on forever. Being with him was being in a kind of prison; but it had also been *safe*. I wrote that statement from a place of grief and loss. But I don't even think I knew anymore what I really felt and thought, so I fell back on saying what I thought people wanted and expected me to say. I'd been doing it for so long that what I should say and what I wanted to say were all mixed up and confused for me.

Only say good things.

I was good at that.

I'd promised.

For a long time, I kept that promise.

But that promise was killing me. When I looked around at the world outside of those mansion walls, I saw that the toxic beauty standards I'd almost killed myself trying to attain still had an iron grip on the culture. I saw young girls making the same mistakes I'd made—attaching their value to their appearance, desperate for outside approval in the form of likes and clicks. I thought of the girl I'd been once, before the mansion, before everything, and how I wished there had been someone to tell me that I didn't have to fit myself into this particular mold in order to be valuable, to be attractive, to be worthy, to be loved.

I want to tell the real story of my time at the Playboy Mansion— the good and the bad, the dark and the light. I want to tell the honest story of my life, which is the story of so many girls and women who grow up believing that their worth comes from what they look like, and that their value can be given to them by other people, and also taken away. I want to tell the story I wish I had heard when I was a young woman trying to find my way in the world, before I showed up at a party, allowed myself to stay, and made the decisions that would shape my life.

For ten years, I lived in a place where the most important thing was how men saw my beauty and desirability. A woman's value came from being attractive to men, from being the most sexy, the most perfect, the most available. There were very specific rules about face, hair, makeup, body, clothes. And because this was Hugh Hefner's America, this meant being the blondest and the skinniest. There were also very specific rules about how to behave. I had to act a certain way. I had to be interested in certain things. I had to be malleable. Compliant. I had to let people touch me, casually, like I was a part of the mansion decor. I *was* a part of the mansion decor. I had to be back home at a certain time. I had to attend events with a smile on my face. I had to make myself available, in every way. There was no wiggle room for my own opinion or thoughts, so eventually I trained myself not to have any. There was no wiggle room to say no. I could say no, but if I did, I would have had to leave. *Nobody likes a prude,* Hef would say, and I could make my own choice about whether to stay or go. After I'd been there for a while, it didn't feel like much of a choice.

At the mansion, the question was always: *What are you offering?* It was a place where everything was transactional. The trick was keeping track of all the transactions one was making. The trick was not giving up too much. At that, it was very easy to fail.

A lot of women came and followed these rules in a quest to

"make it." If they could get a toehold at the mansion, maybe they could get a centerfold. If they got a centerfold, maybe they could make a name for themselves as a model. If they could become a model, they could make a living in this industry. They could really be somebody. That's what I believed. It's what we all believed. And it wasn't just Hef selling it. The world outside was telling us the same thing.

I used to believe that the women who were in Hugh Hefner's orbit were glamorous and all-powerful. I'd see them standing next to him, in the exclusive, roped-off areas at clubs and parties, and I'd think: *They must be really important. They must really be someone.* But then, I became one of those women, and I saw other women gazing at me with the same yearning, hungry, envious eyes I had when I was twenty-one.

I wanted to say to them: *This isn't what you think.*

I wanted to say to them: *Go home.*

I wanted to say: *Run.*

I was twenty-one years old when I found myself on the front stoop of the Playboy Mansion on October 31, 2008, with a whole busload of other young women, all of us vibrating with excitement, nervousness, and anticipation—trick-or-treaters hoping for the sweetest reward. That ornate front door looked like the doorway to success, to a place that could make all of our dreams come true. What most of us did not know was that inside, it was a maze.

And once you went in, it was so hard to find a way out.

So yes, I once promised to only say good things.

But now, I'm finally ready to tell the truth.

CHAPTER 1

Trick or Treat

Everywhere I looked there were sexy cats. White cats, black cats, pink cats. There were also lions, cheetahs, panthers, and even a zebra. A zebra isn't in the cat family, but this one was certainly sexy enough to be.

Interspersed with the felines were doctors and nurses—each one more naked than the last. One wore just a stethoscope.

L.A. evenings are warm, even in October, but the parking garage was echoing and chilly. I rubbed my bare arms to warm up a bit and shifted from side to side—my feet were starting to hurt. I was so nervous it felt like there were a million butterflies in my chest, or maybe there were woodpeckers. I borrowed a tiny folding mirror to check my face and hair for the thousandth time.

"You look fine," my new friend said impatiently, but then she grabbed the mirror back from me. She studied her perfectly made-up face and her perfectly parted jet-black hair and then snapped the mirror shut and sighed.

"We've been waiting *forever*," she said. "Hey, hey!" she yelled, waving to the guy with the clipboard who'd been fending off questions for the past forty-five minutes. "Is this bus ever coming?"

He ignored her.

My new friend Allie made a very sexy Pocahontas, with a tan, faux suede push-up bra and a barely-there fringed skirt hanging on her hips, showing off her flat, tanned stomach. It didn't cross either of our minds that we shouldn't be wearing indigenous culture as a costume—the "native American princess" getup was still a standard on the Halloween racks of sexy options, and *sexy* was the requirement. I'd dressed as a French maid, also sexy. My costume consisted of a black-and-white satin push-up bodice and matching bottoms with a little black choker around my neck; my legs were sheathed in thigh-high fishnets with garters attaching them to my extra-mini mini skirt. There was no way I could bend over and pick anything up in this outfit, much less clean a house. My feet ached in my high heels—I never wore them normally. I preferred flats or sneakers, but you couldn't wear flat shoes on a night like tonight.

All around Allie and me were sexy versions of every Halloween costume you could possibly imagine. Sexy witches. Sexy flight attendants. And of course, the cats. There were some sexy bunnies, of course, but that was just being a little too obvious. There was even what looked like a sexy firefighter: just a girl in a bikini with a firefighter hat perched on her head. The truth was, anything could be sexy if you just removed most of the clothing.

I clutched tightly to my golden ticket for the night: a printout of an email informing me that I'd been selected as a guest for the annual *Playboy* Halloween party. I had mine ready to show the man with the clipboard, in case my name hadn't made it to his list. Allie said I didn't need the paper, but I wanted to be ready to prove to anyone that I belonged, that I was one of the chosen ones. I kept reading the invite over and over again, just to convince myself.

Everyone was perfectly made up, perfectly blown out, perfectly groomed; everywhere you looked were long bare limbs, shimmering cleavage, surgically perfected breasts. We had clearly been chosen for the specific look of our bodies, our hair, our faces. There was a particular type of girl Hugh Hefner liked to look at, and we were it.

Allie was the reason I was there. She was a new friend—or an acquaintance, really, but I wanted us to be friends. I'd met her on a modeling gig with a creepy local photographer in San Diego, and she walked up to me and struck up a conversation. I was grateful. I always want to meet people, but then in the moment I feel so shy, like my voice is caught in my throat and my heart is pounding too loudly in my ears. But Allie was chatty, relaxed, and extroverted; she did all the work and made it easy. When she told me about the Halloween party at the Playboy Mansion, and how you could apply to go by sending your picture in, I brushed her off at first, insisting that I would never be chosen—I wasn't *Playboy* material.

"Hey, you want to be a model, right? Didn't you just tell me you wanted to be in *Playboy* someday?" she demanded. It was true— I had said that. The women who got *Playboy* centerfolds were the most beautiful women in the world, the ones whom every man wanted, and *that,* I knew, at the ripe age of twenty-one, was power. Allie kept pressing. "So why not try? What do you have to lose? It's just a party! Worst thing that happens is they just say no. All you have to do is submit a picture. It'll just take a second."

"Okay, okay, fine!" I said, just to get her to stop. "But they'll never pick me. You'll see."

I went home and flipped through my modeling photos. I was supposed to submit a headshot and a body shot. I picked out a few that I thought looked good enough. Sultry enough. I attached the photos, took a breath, and clicked *send*.

The minute I sent them I looked at the photos again, and all I could see were my flaws, my awkwardness. I regretted it instantly, and even though I was all alone in my room in a small apartment, I was embarrassed for myself.

The invitation came only a couple hours later: There were instructions attached on how to dress, and directions to the UCLA parking garage. I had to read the email three times to figure out: *I got in*. I was shocked, but excited. And there was something deeper, a little flame of happiness that lit up inside me when I thought about someone looking at my photo and choosing me. They had picked me, out of who knows how many other applicants, in spite of my flaws. It felt amazing.

In the parking garage, though, surrounded by so many girls just like me, but better looking in my opinion, I was starting to feel a little less amazing. Nobody looked as insecure as I felt. There was an ease to the way they posed and laughed and fawned over one another with giddy praise. I watched one sexy Snow White greet another.

"You're so beautiful!"

"No, you are!"

With nothing left to say to each other, they turned away and huddled with their respective friends. Everyone was beautiful and everyone was confident. I felt like an imposter—an imposter wearing a costume, which somehow made it worse.

I didn't know what the hell I was doing in this garage, but when I turned to Allie to tell her I was going to leave, the guy with the clipboard waded into the crowd and started shouting at us.

"What's he saying?" one girl yelled.

"Ssshhh!" said Allie.

"Go home!" the guy shouted. "The bus is not coming. The shuttle is done for the night. Everybody go on home." My heart sank, even though I had just been planning to leave. I had driven two and a half hours for this party, and the idea of getting in my car and driving another two and a half hours home was demoralizing. Driving here I had felt sexy; now I just felt sad. There's always been a fine line between those two things for me.

He started shooing us away. Girls gasped and protested. Some people booed. A big group broke off and walked away, laughing and talking about what bar they could hit. The night was still young. Assuming we were leaving, too, I spun on my heel to head back to the car, but Allie grabbed my arm.

"No way," she said. "We're not leaving."

"But—"

"We are going to that party!"

I sighed but didn't say anything more. A few minutes later, a cheer went up through the girls who had refused to leave, as headlights swept around the corner and a shuttle bus roared up and popped its doors open.

"All right, get on," clipboard guy said wearily. "I guess it's your lucky night."

I hadn't been feeling particularly lucky. In fact, things seemed to be going backward. I was in college, but I wasn't sure I was going in the right direction. I'd enrolled at San Diego State and declared a major in psychology. I found a great apartment near campus, big, with a lot of sun, and overlooking the train tracks. I didn't mind the sound of the trains—I liked to think about people coming and going or just blowing through town, on their way to bigger and better places.

The apartment was too expensive for just me, so I placed an ad for a roommate. Another student applied, a guy named Rob who worked at a chain restaurant nearby. He seemed like a good bet as a roommate—he had a steady job, and struck me as reliable and fun and safe—a kind of goofy football player type. Then one night, we went out bar hopping, and I woke up back in our apartment with him on top of me, the weight of his body so heavy, his mouth seeking mine. I shoved him off, rolled away, crawled into my bedroom, and slammed the door. I felt grateful I'd stopped it in time; I also felt so stupid for getting myself into that kind of situation by trusting someone and drinking too much. I didn't even like to drink, and rarely did, so I was a lightweight. It wasn't the first time this kind of thing had happened to me—and other times, I hadn't been so lucky. Every single time it happened I always wondered what I had done wrong, what message I had given, that made men think it was okay to climb on top of me when I was asleep.

Not once did I wonder what was wrong with the guys who did it.

There was this guy I'd known in high school, nicknamed Sputnik for some reason, whom I'd thought was my friend, too. He was part of a crew who'd take their cars out in the middle of the night and drag race down the dark freeways and side roads of San Diego, moving to a new spot every time the cops caught on to them. Some other girls and I hung out with them—I guess because they seemed edgy and cool. One night, I was riding with him, and somehow we ended up alone in his car, just the two of us. He parked someplace remote and came on to me, hard.

I'd never been attracted to him—he dressed like a raver kid, with those big baggy jeans—and with his shaved head he had a kind of mean, sneaky look. He'd struck me as the kind of person who didn't really have any morals or kindness. He drove recklessly and did whatever he wanted. And what he wanted that night was to have sex with me. I tried to laugh him off, push him away, but he was rough and held me down. When he pushed himself into me, I stopped trying to stop him. I let it happen. I pretended to be okay with it. I thought, *If I just go along with it, it will be over faster.*

I didn't want it to be rape. If it was just "bad sex," I could just shake it off, move on.

It seemed like it was always like that, though, and I hated it—the way sex could be turned against you so easily. No matter what happened when it came to sex, I wanted to be in charge. I wanted it to be my decision, my choice. But it seemed like I rarely got the chance to make that choice with someone.

I had kicked Rob, my roommate who forgot which room he slept in, out of the apartment the next day. I moved back in with my mom because I couldn't afford the apartment on my own. Her place was small and dark, and I started to feel like my life was small and dark. What was I doing? I didn't really want to be a psychologist. I was trying to be a model, but I wasn't getting anywhere fast. My best gig had been playing G.I. Jane at a comic con. There was something about that I'd really loved—G.I. Jane was such a badass. It was fun, for a night, to pretend to be someone who could command a room, take control, do exactly what she wanted.

I was adrift. I'd had a panic attack in class, maybe because the topic was *death and the afterlife.* I started thinking about my dad, lying in that hospital bed in the last minutes of his life, and suddenly there were these dark, crackling walls closing in at the edges of my vision, and my breath was coming fast, and I thought

I might throw up right there on the floor in the middle of class. I managed to walk out without attracting too much attention, but I felt like I was always on the verge of another panic attack. I felt heavy, tired. I thought too much about the universe, and how tiny people are—how tiny I was. I'd start to think about how we are all just stuck here on this ball of a planet, spinning in nothingness, and I'd feel the edges closing in again.

Getting dressed to go to a party at the Playboy Mansion made my whole body feel like a panic attack waiting to happen, but I knew it was more excitement than panic. I was ready to forget about my life for a little while. I was excited. I wanted to have just one night of pure fun and escape—I wanted to be dazzled. I was already nervous, and my mom following me around as I got ready to go—commenting on my costume, my shoes, my makeup, my hair—didn't help with the nerves

"These curls aren't going to hold," she said, fluffing my hair, looking me over critically. "You should put on some better lipstick."

I could tell she wished she was going, too. My mom was gorgeous for her age—she'd worked at it—but her *Playboy* party days were behind her.

"Well," she said, with a wistful little sigh, "I guess you're about to see how the other half lives."

The mile-and-a-half drive from the parking garage at UCLA to Holmby Hills seemed to take forever, but finally, the shuttle pulled up to a barred iron gate. Charing Cross Road sounded fancy, but also kind of British, a magical place Harry Potter might visit on his way to Hogwarts. A tall, evergreen privacy hedge wrapped around the property. It looked like any other crazy wealthy property in Beverly Hills, but this was Holmby Hills, a super exclusive enclave that made Beverly Hills look a little basic. But as the gates swung open, I couldn't be cool enough to not gasp out loud. I felt like we'd gone through a portal into another universe.

Spotlights lined the long, winding drive, and the low, thrilling thump of bass swelled as we approached; a big yellow traffic sign nestled in the hedge read *PLAYMATES AT PLAY*. And then— the mansion loomed up into the dark night sky, looking every inch like a fairy tale castle, surrounded by towering evergreens and redwoods.

If Hogwarts decided to wear a sexy Halloween costume, it would be dressed as the Playboy Mansion.

Allie and I looked at each other and whisper-screamed with excitement—I couldn't believe we were really here. I remembered the first time I saw a *Playboy* magazine, in my stepdad's office, when I was in middle school. It was propped up on a shelf, along with his real estate books and other important-looking stuff. There was a whiff of the forbidden about *Playboy*. It was taboo, sexy, illicit, and over the line—but there was also a sense of everyone nodding and approving of it. I'd opened that magazine as a young girl and thought, *These are the most beautiful women in the world. All the men want them. They are so powerful.* I'd seen Hugh Hefner give an interview where he said "The *Playboy* bunny logo is more recognized than Coca-Cola," and that seemed true. *Playboy* was an empire, untouchable and unconquerable, and these women were celebrities, gazing out from the pages of *Playboy* like they owned the world.

The shuttle pulled around a circular drive. Women clothed in only body paint held trays of drinks just below their breasts, as if offering both to arriving visitors. We stepped out of the shuttle right in front of a huge Gothic front door. Inside, the party roared with light, music, life, and energy.

"Now listen," Allie said in my ear as we stumbled off the shuttle and up to the house. "You can't be shy or timid tonight, okay? We're gonna get out there and party. We're going to have the most amazing night of our lives!"

I nodded at her. If tonight was going to be the best night of my life, I was going to enjoy it. I could be confident, sexy, and fun. I could. Or I could at least fake it until I felt it.

She grabbed my hand, and we plunged in.

Everywhere we went, there were tables full of amazing food, glasses of fizzing champagne, bowls of candy. Wait staff whisked through the crowd with trays; the thumping dance music permeated the air. More women in elaborate metallic body paint danced on high platforms, their nude bodies shimmering. One of the butlers held a monkey on his arm; guests stopped to coo over it and pet its soft, tiny head. We wandered around in awe, feeling like the kids in *Charlie and the Chocolate Factory* walking into Willy Wonka's magical land of lollipop flowers and chocolate rivers for the first time. My mouth hung open, but I couldn't help it. There was no playing it cool or acting as if this was anything less than what it was: a real-life fantasy world.

The mansion itself was wide open to guests—you could go anywhere you wanted except for upstairs. I clung to Allie's arm as she pulled me room to room like a tugboat and just stared, trying to soak it all in: There was a Picasso on this wall; a Jackson Pollock on another. There was a Frankenstein head that I assumed was just a Halloween decoration, but everything besides that, from the rich velvet sofas to the sparkling chandeliers, was lush and extravagant. Allie plucked a clear plastic glass of bubbly for each of us from a passing tray and handed one to me; I took one bright, sweet sip and then another. The alcohol made the panic subside, and after I downed the glass, I quickly grabbed another. I was going to be like this champagne, bright and bubbly and the life of the party.

We finished our tour of the house and went outside, where the lush green lawns seemed to roll on forever. We found our way through the big circus-like party tents, sparkling with lights, and down to the pool, where the crush of the party was the densest. People were crowding up to a velvet rope that blocked off a row of pool cabanas.

We craned our heads to get a quick look.

All the cabanas were full of important looking men—celebrities, maybe—although I didn't recognize anyone right away. Each cabana was also full of beautiful, sexy, laughing women—drinking and surveying the crowd or noticeably fawning over the men. The biggest cabana in the center was roped off from the others—all set up with a couch and chairs, tables, drinks, and flickering candles, but nobody was in there.

Then, the air changed, became charged like right before a thunderstorm comes in—everyone in the crowd started murmuring and looking up toward the mansion. We looked, too. A group of people was making its way down the hill, and they must have been important, because the crowd surged toward them like a wave as they made their way to the cabanas.

People started yelling and clapping, but I couldn't see over their heads any longer as the crowd grew thicker.

Allie grabbed my hand and pulled. "Come on!" she said, and forced her way through the press of bodies, all the way up to the edge of the velvet rope not too far from the big cabana. It wasn't empty any longer. There, *right there,* was Hugh Hefner, just sitting down with two girls—twins. Security guards and more women crowded in behind them.

I stood there, dumbstruck—it was the closest I'd ever been to someone so famous.

And then, Allie started waving.

She leaned right over the rope and started waving her arms around wildly, hopping up and down. I felt a stab of panic—*What on earth was she doing?* I was embarrassed and about to tell her to knock it off, when suddenly, he spotted her wild waving. He looked at her. And then his gaze fell on me.

I froze. My whole body went cold as he looked me over, from head to toe. He pointed at me and crooked his finger. I could see his mouth forming the words:

You.

Come here.

That moment—me standing there at the velvet rope, him look-ing at me, and everyone else turning to look at me, too—seemed to stretch out forever in slow motion.

There was a break in time as I stood in that thick crowd of people: a split second when his gaze might have slipped over me to some other girl, and my life would have continued on its normal, bumpy course. But this road forked the other way: He pointed, and his security guards saw that he wanted something. Someone.

The security guys moved toward me. The crowd got louder. Someone unclipped the rope, and I was moving, as if on a conveyor belt. I tried to pull Allie with me, but security must have cut her off. A minute ago, everything had made sense—just like at the zoo, I was standing outside the enclosure, looking in, and the rules were the rules: You stay out here, and the animals stay in there. Now all of a sudden I was going right into the tiger enclosure. Alone.

A sexy cat moved out of the space next to him on the couch, probably by order of the security guard, and suddenly I was sitting next to Hugh Hefner, and he was smiling at me—not from the page of a magazine or from a television screen, but in real life. With his slight tan, silver hair, and deep-red silk robe, he seemed like a movie star from another era. He smelled like old-timey cologne. His hand, when he shook mine, was warm, and his smile was charming and automatic. On the other side of him sat the two sexy twin angels, in matching white fishnet stockings with garters similar to mine attached to short, fluffy, white skirts. Instead of halos they each wore a tiara. Even with the sexy costumes and full makeup, they looked too young to be at a *Playboy* party.

I sat there silently, a tornado of anxiety spinning inside my head behind the bright smile I'd plastered on. I knew I had just a fleeting window of time to make some kind of impression—I could already feel that his attention was fickle, that it would rest on me for only a brief moment before flicking to something else, like a sugar-seeking hummingbird. He was saying hello, asking me questions; I had to force my brain to work. *Answer him! Speak!*

"I'm a student," I managed to say, answering his question, *What do you do?* "I'm studying psychology at San Diego State."

"Oh, I studied psychology at the University of Illinois," he said, and started reminiscing about his college days. I could barely process what he was saying. My mind was screaming the whole time: *You're talking to Hugh Hefner!*

I was aware of the twins just over his shoulder staring at me, but with their bodies angled toward each other, murmuring and laughing. One of them—I couldn't tell them apart—rested her arm casually across the back of his neck. After giving my outfit a cursory glance, they both turned away in disdain. Everything about them was aloof and territorial, even a little dangerous. They were like lithe young tigresses, defending their turf.

They were like almost every girl I knew in high school.

They looked like they were in high school.

There was another girl around my age, hanging back a bit and laughing with the sexy cat. There was something about her that put me at ease—she had on a costume a lot like mine, only it was pink, and had more of a Bo Peep vibe. She had long, blond, 1970s hair, parted in the middle and shining over her shoulders. When Hef turned away from me to talk to someone else, she leaned over.

"Hi," she said in a low voice, "I'm Amber."

"I'm Crystal."

"It's so nice to have somebody else who's new here, too!"

I was confused, because I had just seen them all walk into the cabana.

"How long have you been here?" I asked, not really sure what we were talking about.

"Oh, I just got here," she said. "I met everybody last night. I was at the Adam Carolla party, and they asked if I wanted to come back." She didn't say it like she was name dropping or bragging or any better than me. She sounded just as bewildered at her situation as I felt.

She was only one day older at the mansion than I was. One day older at hanging out with Hugh Hefner like it was a normal thing.

I was relieved. We were both a little out of place and unsure. It felt like being at a junior high dance, when you suddenly can't remember how to hold your arms or move your feet, and everything feels awkward. We both had an obvious case of imposter syndrome—it was like looking in a mirror. I relaxed a little. I drank more champagne, forgetting that I didn't really like to drink, forgetting that I was a lightweight. The twins introduced themselves as Karissa and Kristina Shannon. Hef nodded at them. "Meet Crystal." He said this as a command, and they jumped to attention.

They smiled at me with a fakeness I recognized from so many other girls so many times, but I smiled back and tried to make it genuine. I wanted them to like me. I wanted everyone to like me.

"It's so nice to meet you," I said. Hef nodded approvingly.

A crush of more girls surrounded us in the cabana. Security had been plucking them from the crowd one by one, and I couldn't hear what the twins were asking me, so they both leaned over Hef's lap to say it again. I just nodded because I really couldn't hear a thing, and then Karissa, or maybe Kristina, reached over to feel my breast. She pumped it up and down in her palm, like she was weighing meat or checking for ripeness in some produce. Hef looked down approvingly, so I just laughed it off and moved slightly out of her reach. The girls leaned back and started whispering to each other.

"Well," Hef said, turning back to me. "We have all kinds of fun planned for the rest of the night. We can find you a bedroom if you'd like to stick around."

"I'm here with my friend..." I said.

He looked down the rope line toward Allie and gave a little frown and shook his head. *No.*

I looked over at Allie, who was still behind the rope, chatting with someone but glancing over to me every few seconds. I smiled and waved and shrugged my shoulders at her. She didn't smile back, and then she turned away.

She was the reason I was at this party, in this cabana, talking to this famous man who was—for reasons that I could not begin to fathom—apparently interested in me. Without her assertiveness, I wouldn't be here. I didn't know then that separating girls from any support was part of the plan. But a part of me knew instinctively that *assertiveness* was the last thing he was looking for. Growing up, I'd learned other kinds of skills. Like how to make myself invisible. Be polite. Fit in. Go with the flow. Figure out who has the most power, and do what they want. Be what they need. I didn't know Hugh Hefner yet, but I instinctively knew he preferred women to be helpless. I could have talked to him about Jungian analysis or William James, but he was not interested in my mind.

"We're going to head on up to the house," Hef said again, this time nodding at both Amber and me.

When he stood up, we all did.

The Shannon twins fell in right behind him. Amber and I smiled at each other and followed. I glanced around again for Allie, but I couldn't see her anymore. I wasn't sure what I was walking toward, but I felt excited. Seeing all the mermaids and witches watching with envious eyes as we made our way toward the house, I felt chosen. I felt beautiful and special in a way I had never felt before. If Hugh Hefner said to come up to the house, I was going up to the house. Amber and I trailed behind him like moons caught in the gravitational pull of a larger planet. I felt like I couldn't have walked away if I'd tried. This man was so famous and so powerful, and I had never been around anything like it, or anyone like him. People called out to him, tried to touch him. His power was overwhelming. I couldn't explain it. I could only follow it.

Security cleared our way as we walked up to the house.

I knew Hugh Hefner's name was synonymous with luxury and glamour, sexual freedom and excess. He was the man who decided which women were the most sexy, the most desirable, and then he put them on the cover of his magazine for men around the world to consume. *Playboy* was something I wanted to be a part of—I dreamed, like every aspiring model, of being in the magazine. This man was the gatekeeper to that world, and he had picked me. Out of all the sexy French maids there—and there were hundreds—Hugh Hefner had picked me.

We walked into the house, and the Shannon twins started up the curved, red-carpeted staircase ahead of me. I could feel my already low skirt slipping even lower on my hips as I walked up the stairs. Amber was behind me, and Hef, after stopping to talk to staff, followed last—maybe to make sure no one got away. Or maybe he just liked the view. We all wore micro skirts, we all wore skinny string thongs, or nothing at all, and I know I had Karissa's bare ass in my face as I walked up those stairs. Or maybe it was Kristina's ass. I knew we were headed to his bedroom and that it was probably going to be wild, but I wasn't thinking about the sex.

I had consumed a lot of champagne, although I didn't feel drunk. I felt sober and also like I was floating. Everything was shimmery and golden, and I thought that this feeling was what I had been missing my entire life. I wasn't worrying or planning or preparing to be disappointed or waiting for the other shoe to drop. I didn't feel self-conscious or out of place. I felt intoxicated by this new, mysterious, exciting version of my life, and by all the possibilities waiting for me at the top of the stairway.

Hours ago I was pretending to be sexy and confident and fun, and now I was all that and more.

I was chosen.

CHAPTER 2

First Blood

The first time I remember a man touching me when I didn't want him to, I was nine years old.

My parents went out a lot at night—they loved to get dressed up and be social. They loved the nightlife and the partying that came with it. A tired kid is a party-killer, so they pawned me off on whoever was available near our house to watch me. Sometimes it was a woman down the street—the sister of a musician in the Grateful Dead band—whose house always reeked of marijuana. She would get high and tell me about her life in long, elaborate stories that went on and on and never quite landed on whatever point she was trying to make. I think she thought she had life lessons for me, but the only thing I learned was that getting high made you incoherent.

Other times it was a single dad who also lived on our street. He had a fourteen-year-old daughter, and while I don't know what I had in common with a teenager, there was something about her that drew me to her, and we had become friends. She was wary and mysterious, like she knew things I didn't, and at the time I just thought that was what it meant to be a teenager. She wore lots of makeup and always felt slightly dangerous to me, although there was no outward reason for me to think that, and she was perfectly nice if a bit aloof. Even at nine, I could sense she had secrets. And if there was a choice on where I was to go while my parents were out, I chose her house.

They didn't have an extra bed, so I slept on the floor when they watched me. One night, I was asleep facedown, my head on a throw pillow, when I felt hands rubbing my back. I jolted awake, and out of the corner of my eye I saw it was my friend's dad leaning over me. His hands massaged my back through my thin polyester pajamas, and I froze. I quickly shut my eyes and pretended to be asleep. He jostled me a little and rubbed my back even harder, trying to wake me up. I pressed my eyes shut tighter and thought if I just pretended to be asleep he would go away. He would stop touching me, pressing on my flesh like I was clay to mold. I don't remember much after that, so in my mind I tell myself it worked and he went away. I tell myself that he stopped touching me, went to his room, and realized that nine-year-old girls don't need massages in the middle of the night.

In the morning I couldn't look at my friend, and she didn't look at me. I went home and never said a word. Not long after, the police showed up at my parents' house to ask questions.

They had discovered this dad was molesting his daughter and asked if I had ever said anything to them about him. When they asked me if anything had ever happened or if she had ever said anything to me, I felt confused and afraid. I felt ashamed of the night he had rubbed my skin, so I shook my head. "No," I said over and over again. "No, not at all."

I think about that girl sometimes, with her face too young in full makeup, and the look in her eyes that was somewhere between haunted and hunted. I don't have a name for that look, but I've seen that same look since, in the faces of girls I met at my early modeling gigs, at clubs, and at parties at the Playboy Mansion.

I've seen that same look in the mirror.

My family was always looking for belonging, for acceptance. We were always trying to get hold of a little piece of the American dream. A house, a nice shiny car, some money in the bank. Success, stability, not having to worry about where the next paycheck was coming from or how the bills were going to be paid. My parents always struggled to provide the basics but dreamed of something more. Fame, fortune, and our name in lights on a marquee: *HARRIS* in bright bulbs, the opening act.

My dad, Ray Harris, was a singer. He had a beautiful voice. In my earliest memories, he is onstage in a dark, smoky club, standing there with his guitar in a halo of light. He's smiling while he sings, his voice smooth and low and confident. His wavy, dark hair is long, just brushing his shoulders, and he's dressed in a pale blue suit and shiny shoes. The suit is a lot, but he can pull it off. He can pull anything off.

Ray and Lee—my mom—met in England in the early seventies. My mom was young when they met, only twenty years old, but she was already divorced with two little girls. She'd had her first baby at sixteen, her second a couple years later. She was still a kid herself. By the time she ran into Ray, a charming young musician with calluses on his fingers from playing his guitar, she'd run away from what turned out to be an abusive marriage and had a four-year-old and a toddler in tow. But she was beautiful and bubbly like an English Goldie Hawn, with blond hair and an upbeat, energetic personality despite everything she'd been through. They fell in love and joined forces to work hard and create a better life for the family.

In 1981, they flew to California on a one-way ticket. Neither one had a green card. They were undocumented immigrants, flying under the radar on visitor's visas. They brought my half-sisters, a couple of suitcases, and my dad's dream of becoming a singer. They had nothing but that dream, and they clung to it.

They didn't know anyone in California, or anyone in America, for that matter. They moved into a motel on the outskirts of Los Angeles. Just across the road, there was a squat little building with a sign: *Over 21*. Figuring it was a bar, my dad went over to see about a gig. He hunted down the owner and asked if they ever did any live music.

"No," the owner said.

"Well, have you ever thought about having some?" my dad asked. "Your patrons might enjoy it."

"No."

My dad persisted. He would do it for free, he said. He listed all the benefits of having live music: People might stay longer, they might buy more drinks. He proposed that he come over on a quiet night and play a couple tunes; what did he have to lose? Finally the owner shrugged.

"Fine," he said. "Knock yourself out."

My dad came back the following Monday as they'd agreed—the quietest night there is. When he started setting up his mic and guitar, the owner stared in confusion for a minute.

"Oh, yeah," he said finally. "I forgot you were coming." He turned his back and went back to polishing pint glasses.

From here, the story—which I heard a hundred times as a kid—has a happy ending: My dad started to sing, and the bar lit up. People loved it. They sat; they stayed. My dad was a magnetic, confident performer—he'd spent hours in his room as a kid, teaching himself to play, practicing until he had his act perfected. Even though he was really shy as a kid, music gave him confidence, and he never had a second of stage fright in his life. He got up there and commanded the room. Of course, I wasn't there yet, but I can picture that scene clear as day: a dingy little roadside bar utterly transformed by Ray Harris's magic.

At the end of the night, the owner approached my dad. "You're singing Thursdays, Fridays, and Saturdays, and managing the bar the rest of the time." He handed over the key. "Lock up when you leave."

Ray was a huge hit, and one night a few weeks later, the gruff bar owner got curious and asked my dad where he was living with that young wife and two little girls.

"In the motel across the street," he replied.

"Come with me," said the owner. He led him to an apartment down the road and put down the first and last month's rent. It wasn't a big place, but it was better than a motel room. My parents had caught a break. They'd gotten a toehold—the tiniest little one—in the warm dirt of California, in the gig music industry. I wish the story kept going from here in the way that a classic Hollywood story would, with one success after another. But real life is more complicated, with twists and turns and unexpected setbacks, with bridges that crumble under you and roads that turn into dead ends.

When that opportunity ended—they never tell that part of the story—my parents chased gig after gig in California and around the Southwest. I was born in Lake Havasu City, Arizona, in 1986, a place I don't remember because we quickly left, just as we left a lot of places. My parents always had a new idea, a new plan, a new potential opportunity to move us into a better life. They didn't hesitate to uproot us for the next possibility. Movement was progress, and progress was good. If you wanted to make it, you had to grab on to the next rung and pull yourself up, even if it meant giving up everything. They romanticized money and fame, probably a bit too much. That's what success was. And they never stopped chasing it. My dad had a big, lofty dream of musical success, yes, but really the dream behind the dream and the success was simple: They wanted security for our family.

Ray and Lee wanted to stay in America but my grandmother became ill, then after she passed away my dad had the opportunity to own a pub back in England. It was in West Bromwich, a little market town near Birmingham, in an area known as the "Black Country" because of the coal seam that runs through it. The region was fueled by coal jobs: mining, foundries, steel mills. The pub was called Ye Olde Rose and Crown, and it had been around since the 1800s. It was a classic English public house, or "free house" as it said on the sign—it looked like a comfy little house on the outside, and it looked like a comfy little house on the inside. The main room in the pub was crammed with tables and chairs, glass ashtrays, and cozy side tables with mismatched lamps, glowing neon signs that said *Coca-Cola* and *Guinness*. There was a pool table and a little corner set aside for live music, with a low stage and an electric switchboard mounted to the wall. My dad would get up there and play his gorgeous baby-blue guitar, and people would crowd in to hear him.

I grew up in that pub. As a baby, I slept in my crib upstairs while both my parents tended bar below, a baby monitor propped on the bar, the volume turned all the way up so they could hear my cries over the din of the pub if I woke up. Sometimes they'd hear murmuring over the baby monitor that was quite definitely *not* baby babble. My mom would rush upstairs to check, thinking someone was in the room with me, but I would be alone, safe in my crib, tucked in just as she'd left me. My dad had a running bit he would do about the voices. He said it was just a pair of friendly old ghosts he called Art and Mildred.

"Ah, Lee, it's just Art and Mildred," he'd tell my mom when she picked up the baby monitor and pressed it to her ear. "Not to worry, babe."

Everyone thought the pub was haunted—in the basement, next to the kegs and extra glassware, there were long, cylindrical containers cut into the walls, lined in white brick. Hundreds of years ago, apparently, they'd been used to store bodies and keep them cool when people in town died. Maybe it was haunted, or maybe it was an old building with old wiring—often, the lights over the pool table would flicker and sputter.

"Art and Mildred again," my father would say, and then he'd shout to them, asking them to flicker the lights again. Sometimes, they would oblige.

My parents seemed to enjoy running the pub, but they still dreamed of California. They talked a lot about what was next. Something on the horizon was always bigger and better. I learned quickly that what was bigger and better than this place was America, and California specifically, where my father's muffled music career might really take off. In England, it rained a lot, and it was cold all the time. I wore heavy sweaters and a raincoat to school, walking myself to kindergarten through the rain, thinking of California, this mythical, magical place my parents went on about, where there was warm sun and money and opportunity. Almost every day on my walk, I passed a gaggle of geese that liked to hang out on the town green, nipping at the grass. When they saw me, they would run after me, nipping at my coat.

My parents listened to our old radio, and when the Beach Boys' song about California girls came on they would light up and dance around, singing the lyrics together. I knew from that song that California girls were perfect, better than any other type of girl. I wanted to be a California girl, walking to school in the warm California air, with long blond hair and my skin California tan, instead of slogging through the mud with another stuffy nose from the cold weather and geese chasing me.

And then, suddenly, I was one.

When I was six, my parents sold Ye Olde Rose and Crown, packed a few suitcases once again, and moved us back to sunny California. Once again, they were full of dreams and ready to do whatever it took to stay. My mom was going to get her real estate license. My dad would get gigs again. In England, he'd had the chance to open for some big names when they came through to play at local venues. He'd once been an opening act for Sammy Davis Jr. and Johnny Cash in Australia. And in California, he hit the ground running. He took every gig in every smoke-filled hole-in-the-wall. He got his name out there every chance he got. And he drew crowds to any place he sang. People loved him, gravitated toward him. He always had a crowd around him, wanting to chat him up, to be near him. He made everyone he met feel warm and welcome, like he had sunshine emanating from him. He could charm anybody with his smile and his silky singing voice and his rakish British accent and his way of calling everyone "babe." *Thanks, babe. You're the best, babe.* People would hop up to help him out, carry his amps and instruments, even work for him for free, just to be around him. He was magnetic.

I was twelve years old, and I worshipped him.

And then he got sick.

His illness started with headaches. He'd come home from gigs complaining about them—skull-splitting headaches that wouldn't go away. My mom thought it might just be all the smoke in the bars where he played, but they didn't go away. They got worse.

Ray Harris was not big on doctors. He said they were a racket. He said they'd take your money, then shrug and tell you, "I don't know." But the headaches were so bad, he finally went.

He came home looking sheepish.

"A sinus infection," he reported.

My mom laughed. "See? I told you so," she said, but she put her arms around him and kissed his cheek, relieved. Things between my parents had been up and down. They snapped at each other more. My mom could be so sarcastic. But my dad was steady, a rock. He didn't get ruffled easily. And they still loved each other—they were still Ray and Lee. They'd been together almost twenty-five years. They'd been young together, and now they were a little older, and a little more tired. They were still trying. But it wasn't like the earlier years, when I was little, and my mom would drag me along to all his shows. Back then, she trailed him like a groupie. I'd fall asleep in a slippery, cold leather booth in the back of a dark pub; she'd be on the dance floor while he played. He used to end his shows with a cover of my favorite song: "Somewhere Over the Rainbow."

We stopped going to his shows. My mom had other things to do—she was taking a class now, studying for her real estate license, and I had just started middle school. I was wrapped up in home-work, clothes, music, and makeup. The social world of sixth grade had consumed me, and I had homework to do, outfits to carefully construct, and friends to call on the cordless phone, which I took into my room for hours at a time so that my parents couldn't eavesdrop on my critically important teenage conversations.

One night, I woke up to the sound of someone moaning, and then screaming in pain. I jumped out of bed and ran down the hall—I couldn't imagine what that awful sound could be. It was my father. He was sitting up on the couch in the living room, rocking, holding his head in his hands, pressing his hands to the side of his head, like he could squeeze the pain away.

This time, the doctors found it: a brain tumor.

It was cancerous. And the operation to remove it would be complicated. They might be able to remove all the cancer, his surgeons said, but it would be risky. The chance he'd survive the procedure was about fifty-fifty. He said he'd take those odds. He wanted to live.

They scheduled the operation immediately. It was scary, to send him off to the hospital and into this surgery he might not come back from, but he was hopeful. We all were. It just didn't seem possible that anything would happen to him. He was so steady, so permanent. He was a force of nature.

The day before the surgery, he went in for some preparatory tests. One of the things they did to get ready was a scan of his entire body, to make sure the cancer hadn't spread beyond the one tumor in his brain, the one that was causing those shattering headaches. But it had. It was everywhere. The scan showed tumors riddling his lungs and torso. One, in his stomach, was the size of a lemon.

They sent him home. The surgery was no longer needed. There was nothing they could do. *Six weeks,* they told him. But we simply didn't believe it.

My mother decided to send me away to visit my older sister. "Your dad will be fine; go visit Melanie." It was my spring break, and I think my mom just wanted me out of the house so I wouldn't see the hard parts.

Oklahoma was flat as a pancake, with a big dome of blue sky above it. On the freeway, you could see miles in every direction—the horizon was a straight line that just went on and on. My older sister Melanie had followed a guy she was dating to a little town called Gore. He was in the military and had been stationed at a base nearby. Just a few years before she'd been a teenager living at home with me in San Diego, fighting with our mother and causing drama, and now they had a house, and she was living like an adult, buying groceries and folding laundry. She had a whole other life out here in the big, flat middle of the country. It was crazy to me.

A part of me knew why my mom was sending me away for a week, but I went to Oklahoma, visited my sister, and worked hard to pretend my dad wasn't as ill as the doctors said.

One morning I went to the bathroom, and there was a splotch of blood on my underwear, dark red. I was scared. I had no idea what it could possibly be—nobody had told me what to expect—not my mom, not my sisters, no one. My first thought was that I was dying, too. Frantic and embarrassed, I whipped toilet paper off the roll, wrapped it around and around my hand until I made a thick pad, and arranged it as best I could. When I came out into the living room, my sister was standing there with the phone, one hand covering the receiver. She had the strangest look on her face.

"We need to go home," she told me. "Dad is dying."

It had happened much faster than they thought. It hadn't been six weeks. It had not even been half that. It seemed unreal. It seemed wildly unfair. It seemed like someone, something, had broken the rules that we had all agreed upon. This was not how it was supposed to be. It felt like there should be someone we could talk to, explain things, and they could fix it. "Oh, I'm sorry, we made a mistake," they would say, and then they would rearrange the timeline so that my dad did not have tumors the size of lemons in his brain and body, so that there was no cancer and no headaches, so that it was just a normal evening with him tuning his guitar for a show, tying on his dress shoes, calling "Love you" over his shoulder as he went out the door.

Instead, he was lying in a hospital bed, hooked up to every machine imaginable. He couldn't communicate. He couldn't even make eye contact. He could only raise his eyebrows a little bit. It was hard to tell if he was conscious or not; if he knew we were there, if he could hear anything we were saying. My mom was kneeling next to him, hanging on to his hand, promising him that we would have his songs published, that we would get great musicians to record them. That he would still be famous someday. All these promises she wouldn't be able to keep.

And then she turned to me.

"Crystal," she said, "tell him it's okay."

"That what's okay?" I asked.

"That it's okay to go."

I shook my head. "No," I said. "No no no no."

My sisters started urging me, too. My mother was begging me to say it. I think she thought it needed to come from me—his youngest daughter. "Tell him, tell him," they all kept saying. "Tell him it's okay."

I didn't want to tell him that.

It was not okay.

But finally, I said it.

I knew the minute he left us. It felt exactly like what it was: someone leaving. Like a distant, barely perceivable shift in the air—someone opening a door somewhere else in the house.

I could not cry in front of him. I knew he was gone, but still, I didn't want him to see me cry. I slammed out of the room and started running, racing down the fluorescent halls like a rat in a maze, desperate to get out. I had no idea where I was going, I just turned this way and that way, rushing past carts piled with supplies; past open doorways with other people lying there, sick and maybe dying, with their families gathered around just like ours; past nurses in blue scrubs who stepped out of my way, staring at the wailing girl who was flying down the corridor like a comet, until finally there was a door, and I slammed through it into the warm darkness of a parking lot. The sun was setting, and the sky was a soft purple. I put my back against the hot brick hospital wall and slid down it. I just wanted to feel the ground under me, solid.

I still hadn't told my mom I had gotten my first period. I had told my sister about the blood on our way to California from Oklahoma, and she had explained everything. I didn't want to be a woman yet. Being a woman meant pain and blood. It meant watching someone you love die. It meant grief and lies and loss.

I sat there for a long time while the sunset drained away and the sky went totally dark, trying to stop sobbing. My chest ached; my throat hurt. I tried to slow my breathing down. I tried, for just a minute, to not think. To not think about what had just happened. To not think about how the life I'd thought I was going to have had snapped off like a thin branch. Gone. To think only about the smell of warm asphalt and gasoline in the parking lot. To think only about the rough brick against my back.

And then, just above me, a single light bulb in a row of lights flickered—on and off, on and off. I remembered Art and Mildred, the ghosts from our old pub that my dad used to joke about. I thought this could somehow be him, sending me a signal. The lights flickered on and off again, deliberately, it seemed. It *was* him. I wasn't sure exactly how to put it into words—whether it was *I love you* or *I'm here* or *I'll be with you,* but I felt it. I knew it was real.

He was gone, but I knew he was still with me, and this thought, this perhaps magical thinking of a now fatherless daughter, got me up off the ground and gave me small comfort. I dried my eyes and walked back to join my family.

Everything had changed, but I shoved the pain down.

Because I was a woman now, and that's what women do.

I didn't know much, but I already knew that.

CHAPTER 3

Awkward Teenage Blues

I lost my dad, and then my mom lost herself.

With my dad gone, everything fractured. It was like removing a weight from a set of scales that had been precisely balanced. He'd always been the calm in the chaos, the one who kept us steady. His absence left us tilted, scrambling. My world dimmed, as if all the sunshine were behind a window and now the shade was pulled down.

Now it was just my mom and me, and we were struggling to survive our loss and, alongside the grief, to survive financially. We immediately had to move out of our apartment and into a single bedroom in another family's house, which we rented for $400 a month. I had always felt like a bit of an outsider, and as we hunkered down inside that one room holding all our belongings, listening to the sounds of another family going about their lives together, I felt untethered and adrift. I lay in that room and realized that everything we owned smelled like someone else's unfamiliar cooking. When I put my head down on my arms at school, closing my eyes for a minute to take a break from everything, even my own sweater didn't smell like myself, like my own home. It was a constant reminder that we didn't belong anywhere, that we were out of place and lost—not a real family, just the leftover scraps of one.

Living in that tiny bedroom, my mom was physically right next to me, sleeping in the same queen-size bed, but in every other way she was a million miles away. She cried constantly. She slept. She still didn't have her green card, and we were out of money. It felt like we were completely alone in the world—she was all I had, and I knew she was doing the best she could, but she was barely there, just the hollow shape of a person. I wanted to scream at her to snap out of it, get up, pull herself together—and then, one day, she did. She got up, did her makeup and hair, and threw herself into dating.

I know she was in survival mode, and that left little room to see what I needed. I just wanted her to tell me it was all going to be okay, that the world was a safe place. I wanted to feel like a family again.

I wanted a mother, but she wanted a new man.

First she dated a string of younger guys—hot and fun, the kind of guys who wanted to go clubbing and stay out all night. Many of them were from the local military base. Then she pivoted to older, richer men, and two years after my dad died, she married one of them. His name was Lyle, and he was a sports announcer and also a writer for the *San Diego Tribune*. Lyle was rich, or at least seemed so to me, because he owned a townhouse in La Jolla Village and drove a Mercedes. He kept his salt-and-pepper hair cut close to hide the fact that he was balding, and he had an oversize ego that had to be protected at all costs, like an overinflated balloon that might pop at any moment. I was intimidated by him, and impressed by his job talking about ice hockey games—you could turn on the radio and hear his voice. I thought he was famous, and he seemed wealthy and classy, and so everything he did had this shine of what

I assumed was high class—including his home office, right off the kitchen, where he kept his huge collection of *Playboy* magazines.

The shelves were filled with them—displayed prominently in wooden magazine holders, which were angled out with a half cut-out front, so that you could see just the word *Playboy* on the cover. I would pull them out just a little bit and quickly look at the covers. All the women shared the same qualities: They were gorgeous, with perfect, sleek bodies and huge, gravity-defying breasts. They were mostly blond, and they looked thrilled to be there, like there was nothing better than to be displayed on the cover of that magazine. That was the look they all wore on their faces: *I exist for you.* To me it looked like they all knew a secret that I didn't.

They were real women with real power.

Lyle thought *Playboy* was the height of culture and refinement, and my mother didn't seem to disagree. If she was bothered by his office full of nude women, she never let on. She went along with what Lyle wanted. I watched, and at thirteen, I learned that the best way to survive in the world was to be appealing to men.

We moved in with Lyle, which meant his daughter Bailey and I had to share a room. I slept in Bailey's bunk bed, on Bailey's princess sheets. I had almost nothing of my own there—it wasn't my house, and it never felt like a home. Lyle treated my mom and me like we were a burden, like we were parasites living off his largesse, and so that's how I felt. Like a burden. Like something disgusting on his loafer that he wanted to scrape off. He was fastidious and highly organized, and would point it out immediately if I left a dish in the sink or my backpack on the floor. His own daughter could make any kind of mess she wanted, but not me. So I tried hard to not take up too much space or bother anyone.

On the first day of high school in La Jolla, I put my outfit together carefully. My mom had taken me shopping, and I'd picked out a denim-on-denim Xhilaration brand ensemble. It was cheap, because that's what we could afford, but I thought it was cool. As soon as I walked into the cool air-conditioned building, where expensive perfume hung in the air, I understood how horribly wrong I was. The other girls were dressed in designer clothes and carried expensive designer bags. They proudly wore their Frankie B jeans with Rocket Dog sandals. Frankie B's were expensive, the brand started by the wife of the guitarist from Guns N' Roses, who named the company after their daughter. I couldn't imagine having a clothing line named after me, and I imagined Frankie's fabulous life. Rocket Dogs weren't that expensive, but were still out of my budget. Kids twirled the keys to their parents' sports cars on their fingers. The kids at my school had anything they wanted, including expensive, high-end drugs. The other girls took one look at my department-store outfit and laughed.

Just about every weekend, there was a party at somebody's mansion, which their parents had left them alone in while they flew off to some exotic vacation. I would wander through those huge, fancy houses with every amenity you could think of, movie rooms and glittering pools and endless lawns, and think, *These people are horrible, mean and cruel, they take this all for granted—why do they have so much?* I was a nice person; I tried to be kind. What did I have to do to have even a fraction of this? I didn't need a mansion. All I wanted was a real home, a place to feel safe, a place where I belonged.

Instead, I was floating, with no real sense of who I was, trying to fit myself into whatever mold I needed to. Whatever the world required of me in order for me to be accepted, I would do it. I would *be* it.

I'd seen those women on the cover of *Playboy* in Lyle's office. On television I saw Jenny McCarthy, Anna Nicole Smith, and Pamela Anderson, these gorgeous bombshell blondes with lush cleavage who had the world at their feet. Pamela Anderson—now that was a mold I could fit myself into. She seemed perfect, the ideal woman. And people loved her. I plucked my eyebrows into the thinnest arch, just like hers. I did my lipstick like hers. I desperately wanted to bleach my hair, since, tragically, I'd been born with reddish-brown hair, but my mom said no. She let me get Sun-In from the drugstore, that lemon-smelling stuff you spritz on your hair and then sit outside, hoping that it tints your dark strands just a little lighter. In desperation, I started pouring the whole bottle out on my head. It turned my brown hair lighter, but also more orange. I used so much Sun-In my scalp blistered and burned, but I didn't care.

I spent my clothing allowance on tight jeans that rode low on my hips, crop tops, sexy short dresses, and cheap drugstore makeup. There was nothing I could do about what I saw as my worst feature—my B cup breasts. I bought Victoria's Secret push-up bras, but even Victoria couldn't transform them into what they needed to be. I started slipping silicone pads called "chicken cutlets" into my push-up bra, but I felt like a fraud. Even after all this effort—the hair, the eyebrows, the makeup, the clothes, and even with chicken cutlets tucked into my shirt—I still felt wrong. I felt ugly. I felt like I would never be good enough or pretty enough.

I dreamed of being just like the other girls in my high school, the ones who seemed to effortlessly have the things I longed for, not just the home and clothes and looks, but the ability to walk around in this life as if they belonged. They had a confidence I desperately looked for on the discount shelves at drugstores and envied on the pages of Lyle's *Playboy* magazines.

Most of all, they were happy and carefree and seemed so sure that the world was a good and kind place full of good and kind people.

They were all Baileys, and I was always the awkward girl being chased by geese.

I was also a virgin, and at fourteen I desperately wanted not to be. Maybe this was going to be the magic thing that made me a different person. I had watched my mom use her sexuality as a tool, and I heard the other girls talking about having sex, so it felt like yet another world I was being kept out of.

All I knew about sex was that the first time was going to hurt, and there would be blood. I wasn't so worried about pain or blood, but I didn't want to experience either with someone I was having sex with. That seemed more mortifying to me than actually being naked and doing the deed. I wanted to be cool and sexy and beautiful the first time, not worried about bleeding on someone's sheets.

I decided the best way to control for possible embarrassment was to de-virginize myself first. I couldn't talk to my mom about it, and my older sisters were too far away and caught up in their own lives to help me with this problem. Plus it wasn't the sort of thing we talked about easily, or ever. I waited until everyone was out of the house and then went into the bathroom, where I could lock the door. I turned on the shower and stripped down. I didn't like to look at my body in the mirror, so I quickly got in the water. My hands were shaking as I picked up the small squeeze bottle of shower gel. It was pink with tiny daisy-like flowers on it. I squirted some in my left hand and then popped the flip-top lid into place with my right thumb. I pressed down on it tightly and hoped it was sealed enough that it wouldn't pop open. I soaped up my body between my legs and then I coated the bottle itself with its own gel. I took a deep breath and then I inserted the bottle as far as I could. It scraped and hurt, but I pushed it in as far as it would go, then I took a deep breath and pushed it in even farther. When I pulled it out, there was blood on the lid and more blood running down my leg. I dropped it and sat down in the shower, letting the warm water run across my back and shoulders. I waited to see if I felt any different, but all I felt was the stinging of the gel inside me.

With the messy part out of the way, I decided to do it for real with Liam. He was the stepbrother of a kid in my grade, and we started going together, which didn't mean much of anything at the time. We'd talk on the phone, but the conversation was full of awkward pauses, and he never really asked me out on a proper date. We'd just meet up at house parties, but even so, I considered him my boyfriend. I was the one who brought up the topic of sex, and he seemed reserved and shy about it. "Please," I'd say, "let's just do it, it will be great."

It wasn't great. It wasn't bad, but it wasn't much of anything, and it was over in a few minutes. Liam was quiet after, so I was quiet, and we were both awkward. But I was happy. I had a boyfriend officially, I was a woman, and maybe I was even in love. I didn't know what love was supposed to feel like, so this vague feeling would have to do. I wanted Liam to tell me he loved me, that he'd never leave me, that I was his best girl in the world.

But Liam wasn't much of a talker, and the longest conversation we ever had was when he called me to tell me he had cheated on me with a girl from church and was breaking up with me.

I hung up the phone just as my mom brought out my birthday cake. She immediately got out her camera to capture me blowing out the candles and making a wish, but all she got was a picture of me crying onto a cake that read *Happy 15th Birthday*.

I didn't make a wish.

CHAPTER 4

True Love

Liam couldn't just break up with me and be done with it, or tell people that he had cheated on me, so he told his stepbrother that we broke up because I was sleeping around. In truth, apart from the gel bottle, I had only slept with him. But I was branded a slut, and high school for the next year became a whole new level of hell for me. A girl even keyed the word *whore* into my car, only she misspelled it as *hoar*, which made it somehow even worse.

And then I met Greg.

Greg was like a beam of sunlight. He smiled with his whole face, showing all of his white teeth. His light brown hair was cut short, and he looked like a younger and taller Mark Wahlberg. Even in the whirling social rapids of high school, he managed to be kind to everybody, and everybody adored him. And he was like me—he didn't live in La Jolla proper, or come from money. We both lived on the other side of the highway, away from the sandy beaches lined with glittering mansions with views of the rolling blue waves. Because his parents owned a bike shop just down the street from the school, he was able to register with that address. Both of us got a great education in La Jolla, even if it was hard to have nothing while everyone else seemed to have everything. Material things didn't matter to Greg. He didn't care what people had or didn't have. He saw the good in everyone and forgave the bad. I had never met someone so sure of who they were in the world—so confident and unswayed by other people's opinions. People were drawn to Greg in a way I had only ever seen before with my dad. Everyone wanted to be his friend. Greg and I gravitated toward each other like magnets, and from the beginning, we were inseparable. He was one year older than me, but we had the same birthday: April 29.

It seemed like fate.

I was happy with him. I felt safe. I could be myself. I could be goofy and nerdy and hang out with him in sweatpants and no makeup. He made me feel like the most special person in the world. With Greg I felt beautiful. With Greg I was beautiful. I fell in love with him completely and utterly, and every moment we spent together was full of laughter and joy.

Every single day was an adventure for Greg. He always had somewhere he wanted us to explore, a place to hike, a little food truck to eat at, a beach cave he had found. "Let's go," he would say to me, grinning like he had the best surprise in the world for me. And he did. The best surprise was how he could make the most ordinary things in life feel extraordinary.

We were best friends. And we couldn't get enough of each other. We always had something to talk about, and we made love as often as we could. Sex with Greg made me ashamed I had ever cried about Liam. Greg was my first love in every sense of the word. When I was with him it was like the world became full of colors I had never seen before. He knew everything about me—my fears, my insecurities, every inch of my body—and he only loved me more with each revelation. It didn't matter that my chest wasn't huge, or my hair not the perfect shade of California blond.

The only downside to our relationship was that his parents didn't like me. They were much stricter than my mom, and they felt I was a bad influence. We weren't doing anything wrong except for wanting to be with each other all the time. I think his dad must have seen how in love we were, how serious we were about each other, and that's why he didn't like me. I didn't smoke or drink or do drugs, so I didn't feel like a bad influence. I didn't get it, but it hurt. What was so wrong with me? Greg assured me it wasn't about me, but it felt personal. It felt like all my worst fears about my own worth had come true.

I was just a girl who wanted to hang out with my boyfriend. My mom, always the cool mom who preferred to act more like my best girlfriend than a parent, would drive me to Greg's home late at night and help him sneak out. She'd drop us off at the beach so we could run out into the surf in the moonlight, the water warm on our ankles, or she'd let us come back to our house and stay up late watching movies and eating snacks. By then, she'd gotten her green card and left Lyle, that fussy man who wanted to wipe any trace of us off of his pristine marble countertops, and she and I were living in a little one-bedroom apartment of our own. She gave me the bedroom and helped me decorate it with posters all over the walls and my own phone so I could talk to Greg even when his parents made him stay in. She slept on the couch.

One day, though, Greg's parents found out that we'd been sneaking him out. They nailed his window shut and told him he couldn't see me anymore.

We hung out anyway—our bond was a tight one. We were star-crossed lovers, like Romeo and Juliet. And his parents trying to keep us apart just made us want to be together more. We snuck out to see each other whenever we could, and would make love frantically in his car because we didn't know when we'd be together again. He had a Volkswagen bug, old and beige and small, but we found a way to be together in that tiny car. After we made love we'd drive through the streets of San Diego, and I knew that I would go anywhere with him for as long as I lived. He was my person, my shining star, my reward for all the hard times of my childhood. Sometimes we'd drive at night, listening to the songs my dad used to play, and I'd see a streetlight flickering, and I'd know it was my dad, happy for me that I'd found true love, telling me he approved.

It was magic and blissful. And then I got pregnant.

After his parents kept us apart, we weren't always as careful when we were together. I wasn't even seventeen yet, and there was no way we were ready to have a baby together. We made an appointment at Planned Parenthood and didn't tell our families. I was given an IV of medication, so the abortion itself was a blur of people talking to me and then the muffled noise of machinery. When it was over I had a juice box and then Greg took me home. We didn't talk about it too much, but everything felt different between us. Greg was concerned about me, but I was distant. Our sweet, pure love felt suddenly complicated, and I began to believe his parents were right about me. I was a bad influence. I was irresponsible. There was something wrong with me. I was worthless. Useless. Less than everyone I went to school with. Everyone I met.

These negative thoughts ran in an endless loop in my head after the abortion. I would look in the mirror and think, *No wonder Greg's parents don't like me. I don't even like me.* There was nothing to like.

My world that had gotten so gray after my dad died, then bloomed in color with Greg, was dark again.

I told Greg we needed to end things, and then I stopped taking his calls.

He decided to join the military. It made sense, because he was good and wholesome and patriotic and really wanted to make a difference in the world. I admired that, but I still felt abandoned. Sure, we were going through a rough patch, but I knew he was my one true love, my soul mate, and my best friend. We would be apart for a while, I thought, but like in all the best romantic movies and fairytales, we would find our way back to each other.

Greg went away to boot camp and then was quickly deployed to Afghanistan. I deployed also, but differently, into a world of self-destruction.

That world was called Owen.

Owen was eight years older than me, twenty-five to my seventeen, and had his own house in La Jolla. I met him shortly after Greg left. His parties were legendary at my high school, but I had never gone to one before. He was older and kind of sleazy and had a reputation for hitting on all the girls, but the fact that he supplied alcohol and a house free of parental supervision made anything he did forgivable. Owen gave me attention at a time when I had no one. I was heartbroken and alone. Greg had been my safety net in the world, and without him I was lost and hungry for any kind of love I could get. That first night he flirted with me and called me beautiful and told me we had to be together.

It wasn't much, but it was a life preserver to cling to. Even though I was still a senior in high school, I immediately started living with Owen. My mom never protested, because she was off dealing with her own failed love life. She never said anything about our age difference. Being with Owen made me feel worldly and special. I was suddenly cool with the kids at school because my boyfriend was the one with the house, who bought the alcohol and threw the big parties.

And he had something else the kids at my high school all loved: cocaine.

I didn't do drugs or like alcohol, but settling into this new world helped me numb the pain I felt over Greg. I was sorry I had broken up with him. It had been such a dark time after I ended the pregnancy, partly from all the hormonal shifts and partly because we were teenagers with no skills to process all the feelings, and we couldn't lean on family to help. By the time I started feeling better he was gone, and that just made me feel bad all over again. I had told him it was over, and he had believed me.

Owen was a distraction, but I was desperate to be with anyone whom I thought wouldn't leave me. I was desperate not to be alone, and playing house with him felt like being a family.

When I asked Owen how he made his money, he told me something about hosting porn sites on servers outside San Diego. They were all in a big warehouse-type building that we'd occasionally have to drive to when something broke. He was always hustling, but at first I thought he was just a hard worker. It was months before I realized how addicted he was to cocaine, and when he pushed me to try it for the first time, I hated it. He and his friends would stay up for days in the house while I tried to do my schoolwork and get to class on time. At first I gave myself rules: I would only do it when I drank. If it got too late, I would stop. If the sun was about to come up, stop.

Owen got me a fake ID and took me to clubs in San Diego and in Las Vegas. He encouraged me to start modeling and set me up with creepy photographers who'd have me dress in a schoolgirl uniform and pigtails or too-short glittery cocktail dresses. I'd pose on the windy beaches around San Diego, up against the cliffs, and try to look sexy, while the photographers would ask me to pull my shirt up a little or down just a little. Owen took me to porn conventions where Ron Jeremy shoved his hand down my shirt and groped me while Owen laughed and took a picture.

I got breast implants because I thought that might help me feel more comfortable in my own skin. Life became an endless seedy party with people made of glassy eyes and grasping hands.

I knew this wasn't the life for me and that I had to get away from Owen and his friends. And through it all I never stopped thinking about Greg and missing Greg.

He'd call me from his base camp. There was always a long delay on the phone—a buzzy interval of static—and I would picture his voice working its way around the globe to me, across oceans and deserts. I didn't really understand that there was a real war happening over there—he never talked about the fighting or the awful things he must have seen. He told me about the other guys in his unit, about the workouts he was doing, and about how much he missed me.

"I've never felt the way I felt with you," he said to me one night. "When I get back, let's get together and talk. You are the love of my life."

I murmured my agreement, but it all seemed distant and hypothetical—he would be gone for who knows how long, and while he knew I was with Owen, he didn't know about the partying, the sex, or the never-ending drugs. I wasn't the shiny, happy Crystal he knew and loved. I had become one of the glassy-eyed people, on edge and brittle. I had traded my bare feet for stilettos.

One day he emailed me a picture of himself, posing and smiling his big, beaming smile.

"I've been working out," he typed. "How do I look?"

I saw the message, but I didn't reply right away. He looked beautiful. He looked like hope. He looked like happily ever after. He looked like peace and contentment and love. He looked like safety. I wanted to say all of this to him, but I needed time to think. I had to leave Owen, apply to college. I decided to write back later when I wasn't tired and distracted.

But the next day, on Memorial Day 2007, the Humvee he was riding in drove over a roadside bomb. There were four soldiers in the vehicle, and only one survived. It wasn't him.

I got the news from a girl I barely knew. Her name was Jill, and she had been a friend of Greg's more than mine; in fact I don't think she really even liked me. But there are always people who seem to relish delivering bad news. Something about the drama of it holds appeal. "Shorty passed away," she said, her voice breathless and almost excited. "He's gone."

She used Greg's nickname when she told me, and somehow this made it less real. I didn't want to believe her. I couldn't believe he was gone. "Where are you?" I asked. "I'll come meet you."

I met her at an In-N-Out Burger near Pacific Beach, right off the freeway. It had to be a mistake. I had just received an email from him. This couldn't be right. When I stepped out of my car, Jill came running up to me and hugged me. And that's when I knew it was real. She wouldn't be hugging me if it weren't real.

The sobs came then, and I held on to her and cried as she

told me what happened. A part of me separated from my body, and it was like I was hovering above the black asphalt parking lot watching a movie of somebody else's life.

I got back into my car and drove around San Diego aimlessly. There would be no more adventuring. No more sunshine. No fairy-tale ending to my story. The world was dimmer without Greg in it, and I knew that my life would never be the same. I had once loved someone so brightly and so beautifully, and they had once loved me the same.

Back at Owen's house I told him it was over, and then I packed up some things, drove to my mom's apartment, and got into her bed, where I stayed for the next week.

I replayed every memory I had of Greg, of us together. I wondered whether, if I had chosen to keep the pregnancy, that would have kept him from joining the military and he'd still be alive. What if I hadn't pushed him away? Would he have still joined the military? I wondered if this was my punishment for doing drugs and partying and living with Owen and being a part of his seedy world.

I wondered whether Greg's parents were right—I was bad, and I didn't deserve him.

l wasn't sure whether his family would invite me to his funeral. I wondered if they would want me there, or even think of me at all. But they did invite me. I dyed my hair dark again, the color it was when I first met him. I stood in the very back. When the service was over, everybody left, even his parents. I stayed. I stood there and watched him be buried. I watched them put up his headstone, which had my same birthday on it.

April 29.

I moved into my own apartment, started college, and took

whatever modeling gigs I could to pay the bills. Greg's death had hollowed me out, and there was freedom in the emptiness. It became easy to believe my worth as a person was entirely based on what I looked like on the outside, because inside I had nothing left to give anyone. If I made myself appealing enough to the outside world, to powerful people, then maybe I could survive in the world. Maybe I could be okay.

I'd like to say that I hesitated that night at the Halloween party, when Hef and the Shannon twins and Amber and I were walking up the stairs to his bedroom. I'd like to be able to say that I thought twice about following them into Hef's bedroom when they held open the door and invited me in, or that I hesitated when I saw the king-size bed or when the large television screens started playing porn movies.

But I didn't.

I was twenty-one years old and had already lost the only two men I had ever loved.

I had already lost myself.

I thought I had nothing left to lose.

CHAPTER 5

Silk Pajamas

I glanced over my shoulder one last time at the top of the stairs. Below us were various staff and security all looking up with big fake smiles on their faces. There was also someone taking pictures, and I had to wonder at the angle they were getting as we walked up the stairs. Amber grabbed my hand, and together we followed the Shannon twins through a dark, red-carpeted foyer and into the master bedroom. It was huge and opulent, with chandeliers, mirrors, heavy drapery, and an elaborately carved marble mantel. It was like a museum of . . . *stuff*. Every surface was full of carefully curated items, evidence of Hef's celebrity and his association with other celebrities. There were photographs of him with people I recognized from television and the movies—Jennifer Aniston, Scarlett Johansson, Thora Birch, Brad Pitt. There was a photo of Arnold Schwarzenegger holding up his arms, a girl hanging on each bicep. There were tons of toys and stuffed animals, and even more Frankenstein figurines and posters. There were things piled in every corner, so much stuff that seemed to have no order or organization. There were glass cupboards full of what looked like VHS tapes. I wondered what was on them.

The entire room seemed to be carved out of wood and marble. There were paintings and curtains everywhere—I couldn't even tell where the windows were, exactly. It felt like being on board a ship, below the water line, as though we had descended into the belly of something.

The chandelier, I noticed, was decorated with underwear. Lacy, frilly women's panties. Like some kind of carousel of trophies.

Hef was busying himself about the room, dimming the lights, taking off his robe. He pressed some buttons on a remote, and music started playing. Four big television screens, mounted into the walls on either side of the head and foot of the bed, flipped on.

"Come here," one of the twins snapped at us. They beckoned Amber and me into a huge walk-in closet, where they were flicking through endless racks of bright silk pajamas, every color of the rainbow.

I still couldn't tell the twins apart. One seemed a bit taller than the other, but they had the same platinum blond hair swept up in the same exact way, and the same bored and impatient look on their pretty, perfectly made-up faces. They always dressed identically, I would soon discover, because that's what Hef wanted.

One of them pulled a fuchsia set off the rack for me. Amber got dark green.

"Make sure we get them back," the taller blond twin said. "These are handcrafted in Italy."

She flicked the hanger at me and swept back out of the closet, barely making eye contact. The sweetness they had shown at the cabana was gone; now they were all business. There was no more performing for the crowd. I instantly felt worried. Had I done something wrong? Did I offend them somehow?

I carefully held the pajamas up off the ground as I wriggled out of my French maid corset and peeled down my fishnets. I didn't know what to do with my costume, so I carefully folded it up and placed it on a chair, like I was in a dressing room at a clothing boutique. I slipped into the pajamas. I stumbled a little stepping into the silk. I knew I had had too much to drink, but it helped with the nerves. The silk was cold and impossibly slippery. The pajamas were enormous on me. It didn't matter. I grasped at this point that I wouldn't be wearing them very long.

I imagined what it would be like to have so much money that you could afford to buy something in every color. The Italian silk felt luxurious on my body, and I was grateful to get out of the tight costume. Later, I would discover that the pajamas weren't handcrafted in Italy at all, but were from a store in downtown L.A. Hef could get more just by snapping his fingers. They were mass-produced and cheap, but like so much of the mansion that first night, I could only see the gloss and shine. This was how the other half lived. This was wealth beyond even my parents' fantasy of making it big. I had stepped into a scene from *Lifestyles of the Rich and Famous*, a show my parents used to watch, and I was in awe.

I felt even more driven to make a good impression, to do everything right. For one night, I wanted to pretend that this exclusive world was my world. I took a deep breath.

In the bedroom, the lights were dim, and Madonna was playing from the ceiling speakers, a weirdly upbeat dance song that gave everything a surreal edge. Each one of the four televisions was playing porn. It looked vintage, like something filmed in the seventies or eighties—you could tell by the colors and the giant sideburns on the men, and all the pubic hair on the women.

The actors were all oiled up and writhing around on pool tables. Was this his idea of a sexy scene? I pushed the questioning thoughts away. I didn't pause to analyze it. I knew that I had a part to play.

The twins, now in their own sets of silk pajamas, hopped onto the bed, so Amber and I followed. Hef grabbed a little black leather pouch and pulled out a set of keys on a small keychain with a light on it. He did this with great care, selecting the correct key, and then he unlocked a cabinet next to the bed and pulled out a polished, inlaid wooden box. He opened it and then reached in and pulled out a joint. He held it out benevolently, like he was offering us a treat. One of the twins quickly grabbed it out of his hand. She lit it and took a deep drag, then passed it to her sister. When it came to me, I faked it. I didn't want to say no, but I didn't like being high. I'd had enough of that with Owen. He'd pulled me into his dark underworld of dealing and smuggling, of cocaine and mushrooms and ecstasy, and I'd gone along with so much I now regretted. I had developed an aversion to substances that altered my reality. Since leaving Owen and except for this night, I didn't even drink alcohol much anymore. But I especially hated the way pot made me feel trapped in my own head. I didn't want to be stuck inside myself with my whirring thoughts, thinking about what I was doing, judging myself. I took just the tiniest bit into my mouth and blew it back out quickly. The twins each took desperate, deep drags on the joint, holding the smoke in as long as possible.

And then it was time.

Hef started unbuttoning his shirt, and so did the twins, so I did, too. Some girls from the party wearing only gold metallic body paint wandered into the room to smoke pot, but when they tried to get in on the group action, he waved them out of the room. I think he didn't want to get the body paint on the bedspread.

He grabbed a bottle of baby oil off the nightstand and oiled himself up. Then he looked up at the four of us and waited. He gave an impatient, questioning smile and opened his hands in a gesture that suggested, *Who's first? Let's get a move on.*

There were no condoms in sight, but I wasn't going to be the one to bring it up. The Shannon twins kind of pushed Amber toward Hef, and I admired her confidence to just jump on top of him. She straddled him, and then her long gold hair pooled on his chest.

There was no kissing or romance or intimacy.

Later I would learn that this was a well-oiled and well-practiced sequence of events, one that went the same exact way every time. The steps: Picking some girls from the party and bringing them up. Changing into the uniform for the job: silk pajamas. The dimming of the lights. The music. The porn. Passing the pot. And then the sex.

Even that first night, even on cloud nine, it all felt odd and robotic—like Hef was just going through the motions of something that had once been fun and sexy. Or maybe it was never fun and sexy. When I'd peeked through *Playboy* magazines as a teenager, sneaking into my stepfather's office, this was not what I had imagined would be going on in the inner sanctum of the mansion. I thought of the photographs I'd seen of beautiful women fawning over him; of parties on the mansion grounds, people roller-skating and having fun. In articles and interviews, he'd always said he wanted to be remembered as someone who changed the sexual mores of his time, helped people to be more free, more liberated. This didn't feel very liberated. It felt more transactional: I want something, you want something.

It felt like a performance, and I was an understudy thrown into the show.

He lifted Amber off and looked at me. It was my turn. I didn't hesitate. *Go go go,* said my brain. *Just do it. It's not a big deal. This is what* Playboy *girlfriends do. Everybody knows this is what happens here—it's normal. It's fine.* My body wasn't ready, but it didn't matter because of all the baby oil. I knew exactly what I was supposed to look like, sound like, seem like, to him, and so I did that. I was very much outside my body watching the show.

Above the bed was a huge mirror, and while I was on top of Hugh Hefner having sex with him for the first time, he didn't look into my eyes once. He stared to the side and up, watching the view from above in the mirror. I arched my back and moaned, but in truth I felt nothing. For a brief second I thought of Greg. It wasn't like this was the first time I'd had sex with someone else, but since him it had all felt meaningless. Owen was a sex addict and, like a poor man's Hugh Hefner, he wanted sex to be like it was on the porn servers he managed. A male fantasy of quick penetration that made a woman quickly lose her mind in an earth-shaking orgasm. With Greg there had been long, slow kisses, a longing and a desire that built and grew every single time we were together. He only had to run a finger along my leg, and I wanted him. My body felt magical with Greg, alive, and when he was inside me and I wrapped my legs around him it was nothing but pleasure and love and ecstasy. It was hot and sweaty and amazing, and we discovered each other's bodies all over again day after day. Greg would kiss my neck and I'd feel his hot breath in my ear, and there was no room for thinking. Only wanting.

This was nothing like that.

I tried to shake thoughts of Greg out of my head.

Here I was in the Playboy Mansion, in Hugh Hefner's bed with Hugh Hefner inside me, beautiful naked women surrounding me, and there was nothing sexy about it.

This wasn't about making love. It was about power and control and leverage.

It was a performance. I was auditioning for a part.

I thought it was about my power.

And with Madonna still singing in the background, Amber pulling out sex toys from the cabinet behind the bed, I gritted my teeth and surrendered to the task at hand. The twins had quietly slipped away, leaving us to do the job they clearly didn't want to do.

So Amber and I pretended, like women have done in every porn movie ever made. Our job tonight was to make Hugh Hefner feel like he was the man. This was his fantasy, and our only job was to reassure him that this was everything we ever wanted or needed, that this was our fantasy, too, that this scene was every woman's fantasy.

Amber and I pretended to use the sex toys on each other. I moaned harder and louder.

Hugh Hefner smiled.

After a while he was just done, no climax, just done. Suddenly he waved us off of him, almost pushing us to the side while he grabbed himself to finish the job. Instantly he was moaning and flailing and flopping like a fish trying to get back to water. His face contorted as if he was in pain. For a second I panicked, thinking he was having some kind of eighty-one-year-old-man attack, but then he just gave one last moan and it was over. It was the strangest five seconds of my life. He gave us each a little pat on the shoulder. "You can stay the night in here if you want to, and you're welcome to spend the weekend with me and my babies."

I assumed he meant the Shannon twins and not the stuffed animals all around the room, but I wasn't sure.

It was a little awkward, the way all sex with strangers is after you're done, but we settled in the big bed on either side of him, and he turned off the porn and the lights and quickly fell asleep.

I lay there in the dark for a long time, more excited than regretful. It wasn't much of anything. I'd had worse sexual experiences, times when my "no, don't" had been met with persistence and the guy on top of me thinking if he pretended not to hear me that I'd be convinced. This was different. Here I was the only one trying to convince myself to have sex. I was instantly replaceable in this bedroom, so there was no pressure in the ways I was familiar with. I didn't want it to be over so I could go on with my life. For one weekend I wanted to sleep in luxury and pretend this was my home, that I was safe in this big bed next to this powerful man.

I didn't want to go back to a life without Greg, to a life that seemed like it was just one hard loss after another. I didn't want to live in an apartment with my mom. I didn't want to be heartbroken and aimless and unsure of my place in the world. I didn't want to be a twenty-one-year-old girl.

I wanted to be a twenty-one-year-old woman, one who wore silk pajamas in a giant house with guards at the front gate to keep everyone else away.

The parking garage at UCLA felt like a lifetime ago, and as I fell into a deep, dreamless sleep, I was sure I was now the luckiest girl in the world.

I woke up at dawn, before Hef and Amber, and for a split second couldn't figure out where I was. Then I realized: I was looking at myself in the mirror. The mirror hanging over Hugh Hefner's bed. In Hugh Hefner's bedroom. In the Playboy Mansion. And

I was lying next to the actual Hugh Hefner. He was asleep, mouth slightly open, snoring lightly. He was just lying there—this person whose picture I'd seen on the covers of magazines. He looked the same as he looked on television, but older, more real, more human.

It all still seemed surreal. I could barely wrap my mind around it. I could feel the dark undercurrent of what had happened the night before—nagging little thoughts in which I started to wonder if I should have done it, if I'd regret it at some point—but I pushed them away. A big part of me was exhilarated. Electrified. I felt like I'd been transported into another universe, yanked out of my drab little life and into this rarified world of parties and glossy beauty and fame and success. I lifted my eyes again to the mirror and locked eyes, in reflection, with Amber, who was lying on the other side of Hef, and had also obviously just woken up. We stared at each other, wide-eyed, half-smiling, half-crazed. I could tell she was thinking the exact same thing.

We slipped out of the bedroom and down the stairs. The mansion was quiet. The rooms were empty. Occasionally a staff member whisked by, carrying trash or opening some heavy drapery, letting in the brilliant morning sunlight. It seemed different in daylight, now that everyone was gone. I felt like I shouldn't touch anything, like it was all under some kind of spell. We wandered from room to room. I kept looking over my shoulder, waiting for someone to tell us we weren't allowed to go into a particular room or that somewhere was off limits, but nobody ever did.

We went through the whole house, into every room we could find. I wanted to see every inch of it, in case I never had the chance to come back. We went through the sunken living rooms with their velvet couches, shag rugs, glass chandeliers, and wood-paneled walls. Everything looked expensive, and a little worn around the edges. It was like a time capsule from the 1970s—like Hef had pushed *pause* at the height of his heyday, and never unfrozen it.

Out on the grounds, staff were clearing away the remnants of the party. The lawn was covered with cracked plastic cups, straws, parts of costumes littered here and there: someone's fairy wings, someone else's sexy cat ears smashed into the grass. All the decorations and props that had looked dreamy the night before were lying in piles, now looking cheap and tattered, like something from the dollar store. But nothing could break the spell for me—not the crappy cardboard decorations, not the stacks of *Playboy* magazines and bottles of baby oil strategically placed throughout the ornate house we'd just toured. None of it could tarnish the allure of the mansion for me.

I thought briefly of Allie; she would have seen me walk up to the house with Hef. We were such new friends that I didn't know if she would be happy for me or jealous or mad at me. I wanted to call her, but was I even allowed to tell anyone what had happened? I didn't even know who to ask, but I promised myself to call Allie just as soon as I got home. For now I was going to just enjoy this mini holiday at the mansion.

I grabbed Amber's hand, and we kept walking. During the party it had all been a crush of people, but outside the tents were already being cleared, and beyond them there was nothing but acres of green lawn and the most beautiful swimming pool I had ever seen. In the daylight the mansion looked even bigger than it did at night, and I couldn't believe this was an actual home rather than a museum. The grotto was lush and romantic, built out of giant rocks with secret caves inside with buttons on the wall that turned on jets and lights in different hot tubs and pools formed within the rocks. It was like being in an Austin Powers movie.

Outside of the grotto was a bar made of stone. We made our way to the bathhouse. All tile and gold. Stone fountains babbling with water. Inside were multiple bathrooms and sinks and faucets that were so ornate I was sure they were made of actual gold. I ran my fingers along the fixtures and caressed the walls; then, through the bathhouse was an area full of throw pillows.

Amber and I sat on them for a while, and then we found a spiral staircase that led down to an underground gym and spa area. It was a lush jungle full of exotic plants, and like no gym I'd ever seen before. There were mirrors and a dance studio and another bathroom with a steam room.

There were elliptical machines that Amber and I jumped on for a few seconds. Then we found tanning beds and goggles that were there for anyone's use. I kept looking around to see who was in charge of this area, like I was in somebody's business, but it was just another part of the house. I had never seen anything like it. This was wealth beyond even what my parents could have imagined. This was luxury. This home, this entire property with its guest houses and bathhouses and secret stone rooms, made the homes of my rich high school friends in La Jolla that I envied look like shacks.

It felt again like I had wandered into Willy Wonka's chocolate factory, but the adult version. It was a magical, sexy wonderland of riches, and I wanted to touch and taste it all.

We ran around outside again and walked past statues and gardens and visited the zoo, where there were actual spider monkeys and squirrel monkeys. Next to the monkeys were ornate wooden buckets with all kinds of fruit to feed to the monkeys. Amber and I fed them blueberries. I envied their carefree existence.

The zookeeper was feeding the peacocks. There was a huge flock of them emerging from the big tree to the side of the house, beautiful blue birds that looked like jewels scattered across the green grass. The zookeeper smiled and beckoned us over to check out the birds and other animals. He opened a cage and pulled out a fluffy white cockatoo.

"Do you want to hold him?" he offered.

I let the bird climb on my arm. It held my wrist with its warm feet and examined me, bobbing his head in a way that seemed to say, *Hello, hello!*

I laughed and baby-talked him until it was time for him to go back into his cage.

We went back to the bedroom, but Hef was already gone. "What do we do now?" I asked.

Amber grinned at me. "Let's order breakfast."

We both giggled, and I was so grateful she was here to go through this experience with me. With her long, straight hair parted perfectly in the middle framing her oval face, she looked comfortable and seemed like she was from a different era. My hair was still overly hair-sprayed from the night before, but hers lay flat, and her style perfectly matched the seventies decor of the room. She leaned over me and picked up the house phone. "Do you want pancakes?" Amber whispered. I nodded and listened as she ordered pancakes and eggs benedict and bacon and orange juice. "No, we'll eat in the dining room, thanks."

She hung up the phone and grinned at me. It was like being in a hotel with room service, but it was a home. I was in awe.

"Let's go!" She grabbed my hand, and we jumped off the bed.

Going downstairs again, I didn't feel like I was doing the walk of shame with my smeared makeup and borrowed pajamas. I felt welcome. I felt almost triumphant. I hadn't realized how hungry I was until every bite of food was gone. The twins were nowhere to be seen, and I was happy about that. I didn't know them yet, but I sensed they wouldn't be thrilled with our invitation to stay the rest of the weekend.

After breakfast, Amber and I hopped into her car and drove back to the parking garage where I'd left mine. Both of us were back in our costumes, now a little worse for wear. We couldn't sit around all weekend at the Playboy Mansion in ripped fishnets and droopy corsets. Luckily, I remembered that I'd left a few bags of clothes I'd been meaning to drop at Goodwill in the trunk of my car. We dug through the bags, pulling out the least bad options and stuffing them in our purses. When we drove back and pressed the bell at the estate gate, my heart was in my throat, wondering if he'd already forgotten about us, if they'd turn us away. *Party's over, girls.* But they buzzed us right in.

For that whole weekend, we got a taste of what it was like to live as the one percent. I tanned in the tanning beds. I swam in the pool. I sat in the coveted spot next to Hef at movie night, where he stood up to introduce the old classic black-and-white film they were showing. I was so excited to be there, I didn't watch the movie at all. A few other girls and I all lounged on the brown leather couch in the mansion's private movie theater. Most of the seats for the guests in the movie theater were hard plastic stacking chairs, except for a second couch that his brother sat in behind us.

It felt like living twenty-four-seven at a five-star hotel. And most of all, when I was with Hef, I was a person of interest. People deferred to me. I sensed the shift in treatment and attitude from the people who came to the mansion that weekend for the pool and movie parties—he'd picked me, and they knew it. The respect he commanded expanded to include me, too. Of course I was still the same exact person I'd been when I'd arrived. But with his approval draped over me, I was better, glossier, more worthy.

The twins had basically disappeared for the weekend, except for a brief appearance during the movie on Saturday and Sunday night, and I found out they had their own bedroom down the hall from Hef's and left the mansion as soon as they woke up. I didn't think much of it at the time; I was just glad they were keeping their distance. I assumed it was because they didn't like me. Amber and I went back into Hef's bedroom on Saturday night, and we showed the new girls he invited up what to do and how to do it. For the first time in a long time, I didn't think about my future or anything beyond the weekend. I left all my worries outside the gates of the Playboy Mansion.

By Sunday night, the routine felt familiar; the only things different were the faces of the girls who joined us, but even those were remarkably similar. Hugh Hefner had a type—blond and sexy and compliant.

I quickly learned that if I wanted to be a part of this world, the trip to the bedroom at the end of the night with all these other girls was the price.

This was the rent.

And I was hoping that if I paid it, if I paid extra even, I'd be allowed to come back again.

CHAPTER 6

Hugh Hefner Calling

Amber and I said goodbye to each other like two sad Cinderellas, unhappy that the clock had struck midnight, or in this case, the clock had struck Monday morning. I hugged her goodbye and we drove away separately, back to our regular lost-girl lives.

Back home, in the apartment with my mom, my life suddenly seemed extra shabby. I'd spent a glittering, whirlwind weekend at the Playboy Mansion, where I'd gotten to try on the coveted role of "girlfriend." And then, the weekend ended. I was back on Earth. It didn't feel great.

I didn't know how to be a normal person again. I didn't know what was normal. I tried to describe the mansion to my mom, but the words fell flat. I couldn't describe to her how it made me feel, so I told her about the monkeys and the gym and the tanning beds and about movie night. I made it sound wholesome and fun, like a slumber party with my best friends. She didn't ask about sex, and I certainly didn't offer up the details. Faking girl-on-girl action in a bed with a mirrored ceiling and pornography playing on surround sound was not the kind of thing you tell your mom about. So I focused on the ornate fixtures and the artwork and the elaborate carved wood in every room. My mom understood real estate, so that's what we talked about.

I had some scattered modeling gigs coming up that week. Since I'd gotten my breast implants put in a year earlier—a surgery I'd put on a credit card and was now methodically paying off—I had gotten more attention for my looks. Some of it was bad attention, sure, but plenty of it was good. I knew that I would have never gotten invited to the Halloween party without my implants. With modeling, I'd been going on auditions but hadn't had any luck booking anything—until after my surgery. Once the achiness faded, the bruises drained away, and I could move my arms again, I went back out on auditions. With my new boobs still feeling strange and tight and uncomfortable on my chest, like a bra I couldn't take off, I booked the first one I went out for.

The modeling gig was for a popular energy drink. My job was to wear their t-shirt, show up at a motocross event, and hand out little samples. As always, part of the job was looking flawless and acting happy to be there. And the especially cool thing was, I'd been hired directly by the CEO of the company. He called me himself to hire me after looking through the applications and photos. He said he thought I had the *perfect* look for his energy drink. And casually, like it was nothing at all, he offered that I could use his L.A. house any time I wanted—that weekend, in fact, he'd be out of town. I could use the house and the pool, and his driver would take me anywhere I wanted to go.

He told me over and over again about the famous musician who used to live in the house before him.

So I went, with my childhood best friend, Erin. At first it was great. We had the run of a beautiful house with an infinity pool, a view of the hazy canyon, a whole room full of games—even Skee-Ball. We slung the wooden balls up into the rings and laughed like we did when we were kids. Then the CEO turned up.

"I happened to be back in town!" he cried as he came in. "I was hoping you'd be here!"

I smiled, of course, as I'd learned to do. But my heart dropped. I knew exactly what this meant. And sure enough, the next thing I knew, he was coming out onto the pool deck with drinks in his hands—completely naked.

My friend and I managed to make an excuse to get out of there, promised to be right back, and instead went to a hotel for the night. But I kicked myself—caught again in the same dumb trap. It was just like every other time. It made me tired.

All the modeling gigs I booked were the same as that first one. I was a Bud Light girl, and I'd show up with a gaggle of other Bud Light girls at a bar, in a Bud Light t-shirt, handing out little samples of Bud Light Lime—a flavor that I tried only once because it made me break out in big red hives. As an energy drink girl I wore a branded tee and handed out key chains. Once, I was a bunch of grapes in a Fruit of the Loom ad. Another time I was a Roxy fit model for a line of swimsuits: I'd go in and try on different sizes, and they'd photograph my body like I was a mannequin.

I *was* a mannequin.

But mostly, it was sticky, rowdy places—bars and stadiums and chain restaurants—handing out samples and keychains and t-shirts.

People tried to grab me, all the time. They assumed I was on offer, just like the little plastic shot glasses on my tray. One guy blatantly proposed a trade: I'd have sex with him, and he'd introduce me to important people in the industry. I'd never have trouble landing a modeling gig again. He could get me into the Playboy Mansion, he'd promised.

I said no thanks. I'd get there myself.

And I had. But now, back in real life, thinking about running the gauntlet of jobs again left me feeling even more hollow and deflated. I was studying psychology, but I didn't want to be a psychologist. I had so many of my own problems I couldn't even imagine adding other people's problems to the mix. I didn't believe I was someone who should be advising other people about their mental health. And while I could get a nine-to-five job in an office or a retail store, the idea felt like giving up. I had vague dreams of magical places and wondrous adventures.

At home in my non-magical apartment in San Diego, looking out at the planes taking off, I kept having the same thought: *How do I get back there?* Being there had been exciting, full of intrigue and possibility. This place, this life, suddenly felt like a big dead end. Modeling wasn't getting me anywhere. I didn't want to go back to handing out keychains in convention centers. I'd had a glimpse of this other path—where you didn't have to worry about money or where you were going to live, where you were a part of something bigger, where crowds parted for you because you were important.

It only took a few days for him to call. I came home from a modeling gig at yet another loud club full of drunk and grabby men to his voice on my answering machine.

"Hello, Crystal," said the distinctive voice. "This is Hugh Hefner calling. I would like to invite you to move into the mansion."

There was no thinking about it. I packed as fast as I could, throwing all my clothes into trash bags and stuffing them in my car. I drove back up the winding roads into Holmby Hills, and when I pressed the buzzer and gave my name, the gate swung open immediately.

I couldn't help but cry when I drove through the gates. This was it—my happily-ever-after, my fairy tale come true, my Willy Wonka golden ticket.

I joined the exotic zoo of girls and animals at the Playboy Mansion. Except unlike the peacocks, cockatoos, and monkeys, I walked into my cage willingly. It was that easy. And if there was the sound of a door slamming shut behind me, I didn't hear it. I couldn't hear it.

Because for the first time in my life I felt like I was safe.

I felt like I finally had a real home.

CHAPTER 7

The Rules of Engagement

When I called my mom to tell her I was moving into the Playboy Mansion, I wondered for a moment if she'd try to stop me. Maybe a teeny, tiny part of me hoped that she would at least try—even though I knew for sure I was going. Parents were supposed to be guardrails, weren't they? In place to keep you from driving off the road. But she'd never really been that kind of parent. For better or worse, she was in the car with me.

She heaved a wistful sigh when I delivered the news.

"You know," she said, with a whiff of envy, "I could have been a bunny. I went to the Playboy Club in London, and they loved me there."

She didn't say anything to me like, *What about school?* Even if she had, I doubt it would have registered. School, I figured, would always be there.

They assigned me Bedroom Number 5, and I dragged my trash bags of clothes in there. I quickly learned that there was a hierarchy to the bedrooms: The closer to Hef's bedroom you were, the higher up on the ladder. There were several other bedroom doors between Hef and me. I was the new girl. I was going to have to prove myself.

Life at the mansion was just as dazzling as it had been during my first weekend. Celebrities turned up regularly at the weekend parties—faces I'd only ever seen on movie screens or in the pages of magazines. Corey Feldman, from the eighties and nineties movies that used to play on the television in my parents' apartment when I was a kid. Jack Nicholson, pointing his famous grin at me. Pauly Shore. Smokey Robinson. Bill Maher. James Caan. Paris Hilton. David Hasselhoff. At one event, the whole cast of *Entourage* poured in. I felt like I was at the center of the universe. Everybody wanted to be here—even the most famous people in the world.

Every morning, waking up to sunshine and the sound of birds chirping, with breakfast the push of a button away on the house phone, I pinched myself, still amazed that this was all real. I felt like a girl in a fairy tale who'd grown up a commoner in the village, but had been plucked out of obscurity by a prince and whisked off to a castle. A tiny little hitch in the narrative was that Hef, frankly, wasn't much of a prince—he seemed wrapped up in himself, rigid and mercurial, and prone to cruelty when things didn't go precisely his way. One morning the staff flew into a panic because they didn't have a napkin for his breakfast tray, which he required to be arranged in a specific way. I was surprised by their fear—what was he going to do if his napkin wasn't folded just so? But I was not interested in thinking too much about that. I was still looking at the world of the Playboy Mansion through rose-colored glasses—he was the head of a huge empire, so of course he should have things the way he liked them. I was completely in awe of every single thing in the mansion and full of gratitude for my new home. I was on cloud nine—nothing could bring me down.

The staff took care of everything. They cleaned, changed sheets, produced stacks of clean towels and bathrobes. They prepared all the meals. I could push a button and order any type of food I wanted. If I asked for a grilled cheese sandwich, they'd make it. If I asked for a filet mignon, they'd make that, too. I could snap my fingers and have practically anything I wanted. I quickly gained a few pounds without realizing it, like a first-year student putting on the "freshman fifteen." I weighed 134 pounds, and in this house that was unacceptable. I might not have noticed, but Hef certainly did. One night when the twins and I were undressing for him, he gave my body a critical look and raised his eyebrows.

"Looks like somebody needs to tone up," he said lightly, but with a warning note in his tone. He gave my hips a light tap, to call my attention to the offending area. Karissa and Kristina, still tanned and slender as the day I moved in, laughed.

In a panic, I hit the gym. I stopped ordering food and limited myself to a few bites at meals. I dropped those offending extra pounds *fast*. It was like a cold slap in the face: There were expectations, and I needed to meet them.

Unlike the twins, who left every day as fast as they could, I stayed and sought Hef out. I asked him if he needed anything, fawned over him, asked if there was anything I could do to help him around the house. He would look at me puzzled—he had staff at his beck and call, taking care of the grounds, the animals, the laundry. Butlers and drivers and security. He had Mary in the office, who managed the staff and all the girls. Mary loved to know everyone's business. She had an opinion on everyone who entered Hef's orbit. There was a photographer to document every single day, and others whose job it was to scour newspapers and television for any reference to Hugh Hefner. Every mention of his name was documented and catalogued.

I tried to get close to him by talking about my family and where I grew up. Once I started telling him about the pub and being chased by geese, but he quickly got bored. I told him a bit about my dad, about his love of music, but it was only when I mentioned that my dad had opened for some semi-famous musicians that he even flicked his eyes my way. I told him that my dad had died, and when I started to tell more of the story, he patted me on the head awkwardly and said, "That's sad," before quickly walking away.

Not talking about death and not talking about anything unless it related to Hef were rules I learned quickly. The rest of the rules of the mansion weren't written down anywhere, but they existed nonetheless, and they had to be followed to the letter. I just wasn't clear on what they were. The Shannon twins barely spoke to me—they certainly weren't going to fill me in. Besides, they lied constantly. I had to figure out whom I could actually talk to, whom I could trust. Amber was back in San Diego, and we became friends, bonded from that first weekend, but it was a long drive to and from her home, so we rarely saw each other.

I started becoming friends with the butlers—they were normal people, just like me, and I could relax around them. Especially Henry. He was one of my favorites. All the mansion's butlers looked straight out of the old-timey movies Hef watched, all dressed in classic black-and-white suits. Henry was a portly older man with white hair neatly trimmed, always professional and almost regal in his posture and attitude as he floated around the house making sure nothing was out of place. He talked a lot about his family, and he was always ready with a smile and kind words. Henry knew everything, had seen everything, but he didn't gossip. He didn't judge people, or if he did, he was really good at hiding it.

Henry helped me tremendously when I moved in—he gave me little tips, telling me what time the kitchen opened and closed, and what Hef liked to eat for every meal. Hef's menu never varied, ever, even when we went out for the night. The staff would prepare his usual dinner of pork chops and mashed potatoes and send it along to the club or to the restaurant. We would all order off the menus of the finest chefs in the finest restaurants in Los Angeles, but Hef never ate their food. They weren't offended— or if they were, they never showed it. Hef's power never waned, no matter where we were or who we were with. Sometimes I felt secondhand embarrassment for Hef. When he was imperious and dismissive to staff in the mansion and servers outside the mansion, I would be extra kind and attentive to them to make up for his behavior. Unless someone had status, fame, or fortune, he didn't consider them real people. He didn't notice them. He could be charming and gracious and attentive, and he could be sharp and cold and uninterested. It depended on who he was with and what they had to offer.

It was confusing and disorienting, and I worked harder and harder to make sure I pleased him. But I knew I had more in common with the workers and servers than the celebrities and the über wealthy, so I never acted as if I was better than anyone else. I wasn't. The twins didn't have the same attitude. I liked the attention when I was out with Hef, but wielding power just because you could was never my thing. My dad made friends with everyone he met and was genuinely curious about people, and he was my role model.

The butlers also helped me understand the times Hef ate, and napped, and how he always needed to have a drink in hand with just the right ratio of Jack Daniels to Pepsi. Nothing was too mundane or minor to be fussed over. The butlers, led by Henry, anticipated his every need—placing that perfect drink in his hand before he'd asked for it, clearing paths as he walked, making his environment everything he needed it to be at all times.

The entire mansion revolved around his every whim. It was stressful at times, but I learned as much as I could as quickly as I could. The twins and the other girls who shuttled in and out tried to take as much as possible from Hef as quickly as possible. They played the transactional game well, but I was trying desperately to make a home in the mansion and with Hef. I wanted to please people—I wanted them to like me. I wanted to make myself needed in that home. I had agreed to be Hef's girlfriend, and I was committed to the idea of what that meant. We would spend time together, get to know each other, date, fall in love even. I tried to get to know him, tried to have conversations like normal people do. But he wasn't interested in conversation, not in the traditional sense. He liked to talk about his life, but these were monologues, not conversations. It quickly became clear that I was only to smile and nod and laugh at the appropriate times. So I did. He wasn't that different from other men I'd dated in that way, but it was definitely next level.

The butlers also filled me in on all the staff's backgrounds, and how long they'd been there, how much influence they had. Every day there were seventy staff members working at the mansion. I mostly gravitated to Henry, but also to Edgar, Regina, Susan, and Elena. There were so many that at first it was dizzying and hard to know who was who. Everywhere I turned there was staff. So I watched them all. I soaked up everything I could, like a sponge.

Mary, Hef's longtime secretary, had the most power among all the people who worked in the mansion. She was tall and bossy, and among the staff and the girls who lived there, it was her way or the highway. She was crass and strong and no-nonsense. She was the only woman I saw in the mansion who had any real power, and like Hef, she loved it and wielded it. Everyone kissed up to Mary because she was the one who would put you on the list for parties or not. She controlled access to Hef, and she was strangely possessive of him. When people would say, "Oh, Hef's true love was Mary," she liked that. She liked being his guardian. I wondered sometimes if she had ever loved him as more than a boss.

I tried hard to connect with Mary and also not to piss her off. She would host card nights at her house once a week for the girls, every Monday. She had a way of making you open up to her, and she was good at being friends with all the girls who lived in the mansion and all the random girls who came in and out. She loved when there was drama among Hef's girlfriends—like Hef, I think she enjoyed the competition and helped him stoke it. "Oh, Karissa and Kristina looked great today," she'd say to me. And I would instantly panic and wonder what was wrong with the way I looked today. She gathered information during her card nights, too. One girl who had just moved into a bedroom in the mansion had a little bit too much to drink and had gone on about how in love she was with her boyfriend back home in the Midwest. Mary had smiled and nodded, and asked her questions, encouraging her to talk about how wonderful he was and share her dreams of getting married and having babies with him someday. "Oh, how wonderful," said Mary, as she dealt a hand of cards, and the girl had beamed.

The next day that girl was gone.

After that first night, I never drank alcohol in the mansion. Sometimes I pretended I was drinking, but I never wanted to lose control. I had to be alert, keep my wits about me. I wasn't going to reveal too much to anyone, because information could be a weapon, and I had to keep reminding myself that no one was truly my friend.

It helped to be in with Mary, and she liked it when you fed her a little information about what was happening behind the scenes. The Shannon twins started skipping movie nights, ignoring curfew, and partying like crazy outside of the mansion, and without Hef. Mary was always asking me if I knew where they were or who they were with during the days they were gone. I didn't. They barely spoke to me, so I had no information to share.

Mary had a little dog named Miss Kitty, and we found common ground in our love of animals, especially dogs. I had gotten a beautiful Cavalier King Charles, whom I named Charlie. He was my one source of joy and comfort, waiting on the stairs for me every time I got home. I loved him and he loved me, and I think our bond was the only example of unconditional love in the house.

One of Mary's jobs was to make sure there were always enough girls at the weekend parties. She was also there to smooth over all the transitions—to facilitate getting certain girls into the mansion and then upstairs. She anticipated problems with the girls so that Hef never had to deal with them. He enjoyed it when women fought over him, competed for his affection, but if they had real problems in their real lives, he didn't want to know about it. That was Mary's job, and she relished it. She moved women in and out of Hef's orbit like she was conducting an orchestra.

She was powerful, strong, and could have been an ally in the mansion, but her allegiance was to one person only. I had to keep reminding myself of this, because she had a way of making it seem like we were real friends, like I could share anything with her. But I never complained about life in the mansion or curfew or about Hef's lack of interest in getting to know me. I confided in her because she required that, but I kept it safe. I might admit to being a little tired, but would never admit to being depressed. I might say I missed my mom, but not that I was lonely. Her job, like all of our jobs, was to make sure that any person, place, or thing that caused Hef distress was eliminated swiftly from his life. No remorse. No looking back. No second chances. It was terrifying.

My job was to look a certain way and to act a certain way. I was now part of the *Playboy* mythology. Hugh Hefner had always had girlfriends, tangible proof to the world that he was "the man." So my job was to embody the ideal girlfriend, and I wanted to do it flawlessly. I was to be happy, fawning, and there when I was needed. Hef's interests were my interests. My interests were irrelevant.

I learned the rules through observation and trial and error: Stay trim and svelte (breaking that one was my first mistake, one I would not repeat). White-blond hair, no roots showing. Light pink, translucent nail polish, nothing bright and nothing matte. Full makeup, but no dark lips. "Women who wear red lipstick look like harlots," Hef always said. I had never heard the term before, but I knew what he meant. Back in the mansion by curfew. Be present at all events. I learned the schedule fast and went to everything: Movie night, where we had to walk down the stairs together, pose for a picture at the bottom of the staircase, and go into the theater arm-in-arm with Hef. Wednesday card night, when his brothers and the guys came over to eat and play gin rummy. And on Sundays, Fun in the Sun Day, where the pool filled up with a hundred girls in bikinis who would kill you for your spot as "girlfriend" if given half the chance. I learned who to keep my guard up around. I learned to stand as close to him as possible in photos, because proximity was power. I learned that we had an open, prepaid reservation at a particular salon where I could go to get my hair and nails done exactly the way he liked. I learned that he would not wear a condom, and not to ask about it. We didn't use birth control—he pulled out and finished himself off with his hand, and if anybody caught something, he had a personal doctor on staff to treat us. I learned that he wore black silk pajamas all the time, except for Fun in the Sun Day, when he liked to wear fuchsia. When we brought other girls up to the bedroom after a party—the way the Shannon twins had brought Amber and me—I was the one to pick out pajamas for them, so I gave them his least favorite colors, like blue or lime green, so the ones he liked wouldn't be dirty when he wanted them. That's how my mind was working at that point: Every brain cell was firing toward, *What else can I do for him? How can I smooth things along for him? What will he need next?*

I completely bought in.

I was desperate to please, to be accepted, to belong, and it became my superpower. All of us at the mansion were desperate for something—power, status, protection, security. I was desperate to be considered worthy: worthy of love and of taking up space, which I never believed I could grant myself. I needed permission, and Hef could grant it or take it away with a snap of his fingers. Learning the rules of the mansion, calculating the right strategy to embody *Playboy*'s framework for perfection—it came naturally to me. I'd been training my whole life to be alert to others' needs, to mold myself like clay to become the right person, to say the right things, to meet every expectation. To protect myself with proximity to power.

True empowerment was a joke. I learned early that being a woman meant submitting. It meant keeping myself small. Safety meant being tucked beneath the shadow of a man's authority. It meant living up to the standards of what was required of me, so I wouldn't be abandoned, cast aside, left alone with my aimlessness and grief and self-doubt. If I could be successful here, I would not only be safe, but maybe I might even have a taste of the power I didn't think I could have on my own.

It was comforting at first, sinking into the routine, memorizing the ins and outs, obediently following the unspoken rules. This was my chance to redeem myself, to shed the skin of that awkward teenager, that girl from the wrong side of town who was never quite good enough to fit in. At the mansion, a sense of belonging was within my reach. I could do this. I could make it to the top where I was untouchable, even to the self I'd left behind.

My hard work paid off, and Hef, via Mary, of course, quickly moved me into the primary bedroom with him as "main" girl-friend. I jumped rank, leaping over all those bedroom doors between me and him. I'd poured myself fully in the mold of model girlfriend; meanwhile, the twins were too wild. They were always running off during the day, squeaking back into the mansion right before curfew, begging off of evening activities like movie night or game night because their "tummies hurt." I stuck to him like a shadow. I think he liked that. And he was lonely—he liked to have company at night. I was exactly what he wanted: a mirror, reflecting his own importance back to him.

And because I was now Girlfriend Number One, I felt important.

Hef showed me the vanity—the tiny little annex that would be my own, the only space in that house that would ever be mine—with a dresser where I could put my clothes. The girl who'd pre-viously held the position of main girlfriend was Holly Madison. I knew she'd been a commanding presence at the mansion and that she'd left under murky circumstances. Her shoes were still piled up under the bathroom sink, and her initials were scratched into the wood of the vanity desk: *H.M.* I was intimidated by the shadow she cast even after she left, and a little unsettled—in every photograph I'd seen, she seemed perfect, beautiful, the exact image of a *Playboy* girlfriend, and still, this place hadn't worked out for her. I felt a tiny little hiccup of apprehension, a sudden attack of imposter syndrome. *What am I doing here? How did I slip through the cracks?*

The vanity itself contained a small desk with a mirror, the kind lined with Hollywood bulbs I could imagine in a dressing room behind a sprawling main stage. A space to prepare before hours of performance. Above the vanity was a small window that looked out to a long, beautifully manicured expanse of lawn. In the center was a wishing well, white like the fountain, with carved half-draped bodies—men, women, and children—along the base. A thick snakelike garland, or maybe it was a chain, weaved in and around the carvings as if holding them in place. The vanity was nestled between Hef's bathroom and his closet lined with rows and rows of silk pajamas. Our uniforms.

The bathroom was massive but dark and creepy. The walls and floor were black marble, as was the open, giant bathtub in the middle of the room. The toilet was black also, but made of porcelain not marble. The windows were covered by thick, heavy curtains. After sex we would all take turns standing in the giant bathtub to clean off the baby oil we were coated in. In a world that was opulent and decadent, it was this post-sex ritual, surrounded by black marble and girls I didn't really know, that made me feel cheap. I wanted intimacy and closeness, with Hef, with the other girls, with the staff, but all I felt night after night was a growing sense of loneliness.

I vowed to try harder.

CHAPTER 8

Why Go Anywhere

In February, three months after I moved into the mansion, we started filming the new season of *The Girls Next Door*. There was no discussion about whether or not I would do it, or any kind of offer from the *Playboy* organization to compensate me for appearing in the show. It was perfectly clear that my participation wasn't an option. It was part of the deal.

Hef got paid four hundred thousand dollars per episode. I got paid zero. It didn't even occur to me that it wasn't a fair arrangement—I just felt lucky to be there.

I'd heard of the show before I moved into the mansion, but I'd never wanted to watch it. To me the real *Playboy* was the magazine and Hugh Hefner, not a campy, silly sitcom-like reality show. The previous seasons had three different blondes: Holly, Kendra, and Bridget. Now it was Karissa, Kristina, and Crystal. I was nervous at the idea of being on television—but flattered that people thought I was someone important enough in Hollywood to be followed around with a camera. I was living a magical life, in a place that was licensed to have a zoo; a place that was permitted to set off fireworks from the backyard. And now the whole world was going to see me, the princess living her dreams in a magical land.

On the first day of filming, a hazy, overcast day in February, a whole film crew rolled in—a dozen people, from cameramen to makeup artists to directors and producers—and I could not believe they were all there to film us—to film *me*. As they followed the twins and me around the mansion while we performed pretend scenarios—showing Hef some photos we'd found, or getting ready to go out shopping, or whatever—I was so nervous I could barely speak. They wanted fun and sexy; I gave them wooden and quiet.

"Do it again," they kept telling me, "but with more . . . personality."

"What do you mean?" I asked.

"Just be yourself!" the producer urged me. She was sweet and encouraging, but I couldn't follow her instructions. Just be "myself"? I had no idea who that was.

Meanwhile, the twins knew exactly what was called for. They acted like rebellious teenagers, saying catty things about former girlfriends, shaking their asses at the camera. The cameras followed them like bees after honey. That was what people wanted.

They also wanted drama, so the film crew whipped up fake drama and intrigue for viewers. One of the plot elements they wanted to introduce right off the bat was a rivalry between me and Holly Madison, the previous main girlfriend. I'd never met Holly in my life. I didn't know anything about her. But they fed me a line they wanted me to say, and I said it.

"I'm not the new Holly," I recited to the bright lights, hovering boom, and big zoom lenses in my face. "She's the old me."

The producer nodded, pleased. "Very good."

When the episode aired, it had exactly the effect they intended.

Holly thought I was out to tear her down, and the tabloids picked up a story about the two of us being in a catfight.

Hef didn't usually film with us. They shot as much as they could with just us girls, and then bundled all his scenes into one day, so as not to disturb him or put him out. On the first Hef-on-set day, everybody flew into a tizzy. Nervous energy buzzed through the mansion. Everyone was rushing around tittering, "Oh, Mr. Hefner is coming, Mr. Hefner is shooting today!" They raced around like ants, getting everything just so.

Before our scenes with Hef, he pulled the twins and me aside.

"When you're on camera," he said, in his usual imperious way, "always be very loving toward me."

We nodded. *Yes, Hef.*

The cameras followed us on a Vegas trip to watch a show that Holly was in. They followed us as we pretended to camp out in the backyard of the mansion in tents. They followed us as the twins and I went on a Hollywood tour bus. It was silly, but it was also fun. This was the glamorous life I had dreamed of living, and while I wasn't sure what was for the cameras and what was real, filming definitely made the weeks more interesting.

The cameras were rolling when Hef called the twins and me to his bedroom. "I have a special surprise for you," he said.

"What is it?" we asked, jumping up and down in front of him, excited.

"How would you girls like to go to Italy?"

We screamed in unison.

"Oh, my God," I yelled, but I wasn't playacting for the cameras. It was genuine. I was so excited. I loved the idea of traveling to another country, I dreamed of exploring streets and museums and eating delicious food and meeting new people. This was everything I had hoped for at the mansion.

"We are going to the Sanremo Music Festival," said Hef. "They are honoring me there, and it's a very prestigious event." We jumped and squealed again. I thought that maybe in this romantic country, Hef and I would grow closer and connect in a real way.

The rare instances we did travel away from the mansion, it was often because Hef was getting paid for it—hundreds of thousands of dollars, plus the cost of travel, just to make an appearance somewhere. It was our first big trip together. And it was Italy, not a quick trip to Vegas for a few hours or one night.

We had all grown up watching *Pretty Woman*, and in the end that movie wasn't about what Julia Roberts did for a living, or even the money; it was a happily-ever-after love story—a modern-day, more edgy version of Cinderella. And in it there was also a clear message that money and a powerful man brought you respect, value, dignity, and saved you from the creepy hands of Jason Alexander's character.

The plane we took to Italy was beyond the means of even Richard Gere as Edward Lewis. It wasn't just a private plane, it was a private 747. It was a luxurious house in the sky; a flying mini-mansion with a hall-way instead of an aisle. There were individual bedrooms with king-size beds and full-size showers with glass walls. There was a living room in the back, where the security team and Mary—never far from Hef—spent their time. It was adorned like any fancy parlor on the ground, with leather couches and luxurious carpeting. The chefs at the mansion prepared our meals and snacks beforehand—no airplane food here.

There were also no seat belts. I was a bit of a nervous flyer, and no one asked us to strap in for takeoff. I felt a spike of fear. Rich or not, didn't passengers need safety precautions in case the plane malfunctioned? How could we be lounging in a parlor, miles off the ground, as if we were untouchable by disaster? Even Hugh Hefner's wealth couldn't protect us from everything.

But it seemed like it did. Private planes flew 10,000 feet higher than commercial planes, breezing past everyone below to stop at rural airports where we didn't have to go through customs. Officials would simply board our plane and ask, "Got anything to declare? No? Bye." It was a whole new world, streamlined for convenience and cushioned for comfort. We stopped to refuel in Shannon, Ireland, and I gazed out the window wishing we could pause and go visit the area. I wished I could put my feet down on the ground outside, breathe in Irish air. For some reason, Ireland reminded me of my dad. We had never gone there that I could remember, but staring out the plane window I had a vague memory of being small and him singing me Irish lullabies. I shook the melancholy away and imagined how impressed my dad would be if he could see me on this jumbo plane, living this extravagant life.

This was it, I thought, *finally*. I wasn't an imposter here. I belonged. I felt important. My dad would be so proud of me, of how far I had come. How far I had taken the Harris name from dive bars to Hollywood, and now to Italy. It was intoxicating, beyond anything I could have imagined. Hef's world was opulence and luxury and adoration and respect, and I was part of that world. Hef wanted me by his side at all times. I walked with him on the stage of the Sanremo festival in front of screaming fans, my arm tucked in the crook of his elbow. Five thousand people screamed for him, and also for me, and the twins, and another Playmate who had come along on the trip. She was trying hard to worm her way in with Hef, and I was keeping my eye on her. She was too over-the-top for Hef, taking her underwear off on the red carpet, getting portraits made of the two of them. She was too big a personality and too brunette to be full-time with Hef, but she was making her best effort.

It was strange because I felt protective of him watching her advances—not just protective of my place or my position within the ranks of his girlfriends, but concerned for him. For all his worldliness and power, he was naïve to the fact that people were always trying to take advantage of him. It wasn't a part he played; he genuinely couldn't imagine someone not having his best interests in mind. What I felt wasn't the giddy feeling of being in love, but a growing warmth, a care and concern like the kind of love you'd have for a friend or a distant relative.

Hef was interviewed on stage while the four of us sat around and behind the two men. "You like to surround yourself with youth, with beauty," the interviewer said in Italian. "Is that how you cheat death?"

I couldn't see Hef's face when he answered, but I heard the words. "I do think remaining close to young people helps you stay young...I certainly don't fear death, but we're only here for a short time and I'm trying to celebrate that fact the best way I can..." Later I saw the playback on the *Girls Next Door* cameras. They zoomed in on Hef's face when he answered, and he gave the interviewer a sly, knowing look when he said "the best way I can..." The cameras showed both of their faces close together, grinning at each other knowingly. It made me uneasy, this look that passed between them, but I pushed the feeling away.

When we left the festival stage and walked outside there was a huge crowd, and more paparazzi than I had ever seen. We couldn't even see the limo that was right in front waiting. Flashes went off, people were screaming. They parted for our security, and we made our way to the limo. As soon as we got inside, they surrounded the car, like a school of fish frenzied for crumbs. They banged on the limo and crowded the windows, lenses flashing, the *snap-snap-snap* of cameras the only sound I could hear. *This is what it's like to be on top*, I thought. *This is how the other half lives.* It was dizzying.

After Sanremo we flew to Monaco and stayed in the Hôtel de Paris. I was excited to explore the city, but when the twins and Mary and Hef's brother and some other staff left to sightsee and immerse themselves in the beauty and excitement of Monaco, Hef had no interest in joining them, which meant I had to stay behind as well. He wanted to nap in the hotel room, with me lying beside him, or at least in the room. I looked at the marina from our suite window and tried not to be jealous of the other girls' freedom, all the fun they must be having. I stared down at the mega yachts moored in the water. I let myself imagine, but only for a few seconds, all the people living their fabulous lives on the yachts, in the casinos, in the clubs and restaurants. But then I stopped myself. I was in Monaco, and any feeling that wasn't gratitude for that simple fact alone I pushed away, berating myself. With nothing else to do, I watched the movie *Enchanted* over and over, looping it continuously for the hours he was asleep.

It was one of my favorites. The movie starts off animated, with a prince who's found his princess, saved her, really, and they're off to be married the same day. But on the way to the wedding, the young woman is snatched from the animated background and suddenly finds herself alone in live-action New York. Amy Adams plays the naïve, out-of-place princess who tries to climb up to a castle on a billboard, thinking she can get back to her home, but eventually she becomes acclimated to real life and falls in love with a man from the real world.

I didn't want real life. I wanted the enchantment. I wanted the Technicolor dream world of fantasy. I wanted the two-dimensional world of that movie. Even so, I still rooted for Amy Adams in the real world, finding her own strength, falling in love with a normal guy and his young daughter. I was in the most enchanting, romantic city in the world, living a fantasy life, with a man who had just been called an icon to the world, my boyfriend. Sure, he was snoring in bed next to me while I watched a half-cartoon movie on repeat, but it was still better than anything I had ever known before. Monaco hummed and throbbed below me, and I reminded myself that this was exactly what I had wanted. This is exactly what I had dreamed of. This was every girl like me's ultimate dream come true.

I told myself everything was absolutely perfect and amazing.

Back at the mansion I longed for more travel, more glamorous nights on the town, but without a big reason to go somewhere— meaning a large payday or a special award of some kind—Hef wanted to stay home. Sometimes he did agree to a trip to Disneyland, because it was close enough that it wouldn't interrupt the nightly schedule. Hef loved Disney, like I did. It was one of the things we most had in common. He had started out as a cartoonist and had always admired Walt Disney's work. I was thrilled to find we had this much in common. We would watch Disney movies together, and he never tired of watching them over and over again.

Sometimes, when I was a little sad, he would suggest we watch *The Little Mermaid*, my favorite movie. I don't know if he sensed my sadness and wanted to comfort me because he cared about me, or if he was just worried that I might try to engage him in some kind of conversation that had to do with emotions. My dad had become a subject of an episode on *The Girls Next Door*, and Hef had shown empathy and concern as I talked about his music, but it was only when the cameras were rolling. I had gotten to play my dad's music for one of his favorite musicians—Smokey Robinson—and this meant more to me than all the private planes in the world. I thought this sharing of my past would make Hef and me closer, but it didn't. I had already learned that sharing my emotions made him uncomfortable and uneasy, so when the cameras stopped rolling, I stopped talking. Not about my dad.

Never about Greg. And nothing about my growing anxiety living in the mansion.

The trip to Disneyland was the best present in the world. It was the happiest place on Earth, and I knew I would feel that happiness for an entire day. I had been there as a kid, but going to Disneyland with Hef was a similar experience to taking a private 747.

Disneyland has a rating system in which those considered "high security risk"—meaning celebrities—get all kinds of extra special treatment. We were whisked around through back entrances and past long lines, safe from crowds, and from anyone not in our protected bubble. People still screamed Hef's name, and we smiled and waved, but we were surrounded by security at all times. Part of the celebrity Disneyland experiences is a private VIP tour guide decked out in plaid, who cost $5,000 for a day. Hef had a hard time walking long distances, so he had to use a mobility scooter. I knew he was embarrassed. He never wanted to acknowledge his aging. So I had all of us ride on scooters with him. A whole brigade of us zipped around on scooters, so Hef wouldn't feel alone. Every need, every desire he had, I memorized them and answered to them immediately.

"Can we stay for the fireworks, please?" I begged him.

I knew immediately I shouldn't have asked. His lips pursed, and he looked like he had just taken a bite of a very disgusting food.

"Oh, never mind," I quickly added. "I forgot it's too late, oh, gosh, I definitely don't want to miss the movie tonight."

For a moment, I had forgotten to pretend that what he loved to do was exactly the same as what I loved to do. In truth I was getting sick of movies almost every night, but I could never express that opinion. I worried this breach would be enough to get me kicked out of his life.

He patted my head like a dog, three quick pats, and then turned his attention to someone yelling his name.

I breathed a sigh of relief.

A couple of months after Italy we went to Vegas for Hef's birthday. There was a special Hugh Hefner suite at The Palms, so we stayed there for the night. We also went to a club that was paying for Hef to make an appearance with his bevy of beautiful girls. Walking through the casino was the same as in Italy and Disneyland: people freaking out when they saw him, screaming his name, and the rest just smiling and rubbing his arms and kissing him for the crowd. I smiled so hard and for so long through that birthday party that the next day my cheeks and jaw ached.

I longed to travel the world and hoped this first year was just the beginning of our trips, but those trips were the exception, not the rule.

I tried to ask him about the favorite places he had visited in his life, and bring up possible places we could go. "What about Greece?" I asked. "Have you been there? It looks beautiful."

Any time I was brave enough to bring up a topic of conversation, instead of just responding to whatever he wanted to talk about, I held my breath, because I didn't know which Hugh Hefner I would get.

Either he would smile and offer a few words back and engage with me: "I love Greece, yes, it's a beautiful country."

Or he would get angry, sharp, and dismissive. "Why go anywhere when you can live here?"

He said that often. Sometimes it felt like he was genuinely puzzled about how anywhere else could be better than the mansion, and other times it felt like a veiled threat, a reminder that I was just a guest in the house I called home.

He could be charming, and he could be cruel. He could make you feel like you were the most important person in the entire world one minute, and like you were less important to him than the rugs that he walked across the next. These mercurial switches in his personality were unsettling, anxiety-producing, and kept me on edge more and more.

But when it came to life outside the gates, his attitude was that we had everything we could possibly want inside them. The party came to us. Celebrities came to us. People were desperate to get into where we lived. We had it all.

I eventually came to understand that part of his quick anger when I mentioned travel, or day trips, or even going on a date like a regular couple was because hidden behind the worldly, jet-setter façade was a severely agoraphobic man. It was ironic to think that the thing we most had in common outside of Disney movies was the one thing we would never talk about: We both felt safer living in the mansion. For him, though, it was also where he felt most powerful. The outside world could be unpredictable, and he would fly into a rage at traffic, at crowds, at having to wait anywhere for anything or anybody. In the mansion he had total control.

While Hef didn't love to go places, he did love to be seen out on the town. It was a conundrum. So once in a while, on a Thursday usually, we left Hef's safe, contained bubble so he could show us off—so he could prove that he really was still *the man*.

Those of us who were officially girlfriends, and any other girls who were staying at the mansion (there was a rotating trickle of them who crashed in one of the bedrooms or stayed in the guesthouse for a while before moving on with their lives, unlike those of us who were in it for the long haul), would put on our highest heels and our slinkiest dresses and pile into the limo. Then

Hef would slide in, wearing his going-out jacket with the black silk lapels.

He carried a disposable camera, the kind you could get at any drugstore, and encouraged us to pose for him. He wanted us to flash the camera, pull up our skirts, spread our legs, show everything. A lot of girls did, and I watched as those cameras filled up with the most incriminating images—rolls and rolls of potential blackmail, if he ever wanted to use it that way. He also kept a little black book where he wrote down the names of every single woman who went up to the bedroom. And I'd recently discovered little spy holes on either side of the big televisions at the foot of the bed, where one might set up cameras. When I asked him about them, he just shrugged.

"But what are they for?" I asked.

"I used to do a lot of filming," he said proudly. "VHS. I had hours of video, hundreds of sexy tapes."

"Did people know you were filming?" I could only imagine what, and *who*, was on those tapes.

"It's my bedroom. My house."

He said this dismissively. When I didn't say anything back, he got a little defensive. "I destroyed them all. After the Pam and Tommy thing."

The Pam Anderson and Tommy Lee sex tape scandal had scared him. Hef told me some of his videos were of him having sex with multiple women, some A-list celebrities. And others were videos of wild orgies, also with celebrities and politicians and business leaders, some of whom were married. He only told me one specific name, a famous television host still on the air, a sweetheart in America but a victim in the mansion.

In the limo, I went with the program and posed and smiled and showed some leg, but I tried to keep my skirt on. Maybe it didn't matter—I'd posed for a nude photo shoot with the twins and Amber on one of her visits from San Diego, all of us lying in a pile on a bed, laughing, our limbs in a big tangle, and that photo had been printed and hung on the mansion wall. But this felt more tawdry and gross—the limo bumping over potholes, the plastic *snap snap* of the cheap disposable camera.

We were disposable, too, and we knew it. But I didn't want to feel cheap.

It wasn't long after that night that I heard Mary and Hef talking about the twins. They spent most of their days away from the mansion, partying and hanging out with their boyfriends. I wasn't sure if Mary and Hef knew that part. They were now completely checked out when they were home or around Hef. As a girlfriend you catered to Hef's needs first and foremost. That was priority one. The twins had other priorities.

And perhaps worst of all in Hef's eyes, they seemed tired of the whole charade. They didn't bother anymore to act like they adored him, which was the number one most important—though unspoken—rule in the mansion.

We were on a break from filming *The Girls Next Door*, but I overheard them talking about "transitioning them out" as soon as filming was over.

I was shocked and triggered. I wouldn't be sorry to see them go, but they had been a part of my whole first year, a part of the show, and I had heard Hef profess his love for them over and over again in media interviews, on the show, and in person even when the cameras weren't rolling.

Hef and Mary talked so dispassionately about moving them out, they could have been discussing a grocery list. It was a stark reminder of how fragile my position was.

I knew there was no opportunity outside the *Playboy* orbit for me. I was twenty-two, with no college degree, no job prospects, no real family to lean on, and nothing that would ever be as wonderful as where I lived.

These thoughts rolled through my head, and it was confusing. I had anxiety about being tossed out, about being abandoned by Hef. At the same time I was also anxious because I was feeling increasingly claustrophobic and having a harder and harder time hiding it, especially while we were on a break from filming. I smiled on the outside, but inside I could feel little surges of resentment growing, and the more I pushed that away, the more anxiety I felt.

I started getting paranoid. I had no privacy; any phone call I made from the vintage phone on the desk in the vanity could be easily heard—there was a vent on the ceiling that connected to the floors above, and a noticeable gap beneath the doors. Hef was always nearby. I never dared close the pocket door for fear he'd think I was shutting him out or that I was up to no good. I wasn't, but I had started to vent my growing frustration to my two oldest friends from San Diego—Erin and Noah.

In the mansion that was the equivalent of treason.

I began to think the house photographer was purposely taking pictures from behind me when I was on my phone—and maybe she was. In a house full of Hef worshippers jockeying for power and favor, information was currency.

I was an introvert living an extroverted life all the time, with no real way to recharge, and this misalignment came out in ways I didn't expect: panic attacks.

I increasingly began to hate Sundays, when the mansion grounds filled with adoring women waiting for him to appear. The panic attacks I'd first had after Greg died, where I'd feel like I was dying and fading away into nothingness, always seemed to threaten me on Sundays as soon as I'd pull the fuchsia pajamas off their hanger. I could feel my heart speed up and my breathing get shallow.

"Excuse me, just a second," I'd say to Hef and then go into my vanity and sit on the little velvet stool with my head down between my knees. I had thought moving into the mansion had cured me of these attacks, but I recognized the feeling. I think it was that the "fun" on Sundays was extra miserable, because it was so forced and fake. And because I was the main girlfriend, I had to be hostess to all the hungry and hopeful girls pretending they loved jumping on the trampoline, roller-skating around the tennis courts, and hula-hooping by the pool. Nobody likes to hula-hoop in a string bikini, but we all pretended. Girls also pretended to be best friends when they were anything but. Most of them would shank another given the opportunity, and the extreme pressure of navigating all of it left me exhausted. I'd always been socially anxious, and Sundays were the nightmare scenario for an introvert.

The women waved at Hef and smiled at me, and it was all a male fantasy pillow fight come true, but I heard my name spoken in clusters of women who got silent when I walked by. There were a handful of them who were genuinely kind—I'm still friends with some of them to this day—but even then, I never knew whom I could trust and who was a spy in the house of *Playboy*. Most of my relationships with other women then were toxic and fake. They threw their drinks at me, stole my clothes—one girl even whacked me in the back of the head with her giant rainbow lollipop because she couldn't get Hef's attention.

Of course, she was a grown woman trying to seduce a man with children's candy, so I don't fault her for turning her lollipop into a weapon. I just didn't want to be the target for her anger. Hours in the sun, pretending to be mindless, was an exhausting job. I desperately wanted to make friends, but I had what the others coveted, so I was enemy number one. They wanted my spot. It was understandable. But I couldn't give it up—I had nothing else in my life, nobody else to turn to.

Secretly I was already bored by the cruise-ship itinerary of every single day in the mansion, but I had nowhere else to go, and my restlessness and dissatisfaction upset me. I had everything I ever thought I wanted. I had everything every single girl wanted who drove through those gates, as did so many others who sent letters to Hef every single day.

Once a week, Hef went outside to greet his adoring crowd, with his big smile and his arms open in welcome. His church every Sunday was playing backgammon with his friends while women fought one another for his attention, but we were like children who were expected to be seen and not heard.

So we frolicked and played and acted helpless and clueless.

Every single Sunday, week after week, I could feel my panic attack waiting at the edges of my permanently happy smile. I'd sneak away to my little space and try to deep-breathe the feelings away. I would berate myself internally for being ungrateful and spoiled. I was angry at myself, at this weakness that had come out of nowhere and threatened to derail everything.

Hef had done so much for me, changed my life, and I couldn't comprehend my own mental state. How could I feel like my world was only getting smaller and smaller, when I should have felt like I had the whole world at my feet? So I huddled in my closet and fought the rising panic the best I could, while out on the lawn below me the men played their endless, carefree games of Sunday backgammon.

CHAPTER 9

Picture Perfect

I was worried about my mental state, afraid my anxiety and panic and growing discontent were going to sabotage the only good thing that had happened in my life. There was no one I could talk to in the mansion about my mental health struggles. It would have instantly been weaponized against me in some way. I would have been too vulnerable. I wanted my mom. I needed my mom, but I was nervous to ask Hef's permission.

"Do you think I could maybe invite my mom over for a visit? Just a quick visit, an afternoon maybe," I asked quickly. I hoped it wouldn't set him off, but I didn't know. He never liked to think about any of us having a real life or family outside of him. And I knew if I made it sound too important, he might get suspicious. It felt brave to ask, but my heart was racing, and my voice was soft and tentative.

"Sure," he answered me quickly, and then patted me on the back a few times like a child, which only made me feel even more like a child asking for permission to have a friend come over.

She and my stepdad, Ted, came on a Friday afternoon, and

when I saw her car pull into the sprawling driveway and park by the fountain where the naked cherubs stood sentry, a part of me wanted to run outside and jump in the back seat. I wanted to be a kid again, taken care of, and held. But another part of me was proud and wanted to show off my new world. When they walked in the front door, I could see her eyes widen and her mouth drop in the same exact way mine had when I first walked in.

Hef descended the stairs to greet them, and Ted stood back as he first greeted Mom with a hug and a beaming smile. As she went in for the hug, she accidentally stepped on Hef's foot and then as a recovery move pretended to strangle Hef in a *you better be good to my daughter* sort of way. I was mortified and worried about how he would respond, but Hef just chuckled, and then she quickly thanked him for welcoming them into his home.

"My pleasure," he said.

The four of us stood there awkwardly for a minute, and then Hef cleared his throat and turned and walked back up the stairs.

"Wow," said my mom as she watched him ascend. I wanted to tell her how uncomfortable I was feeling and that my anxiety was spiraling, and about my curfew, and about how the other girls were acting weird. I wanted to tell her I was worried that this wasn't the best place for me. I wanted her to reassure me that it was or tell me to get the hell out.

I wanted to ask her if she believed I could make it on my own, be someone without this world, but I didn't. I watched her watching Hef walk up those stairs, and I could see that she was just as dazzled as I had been on Halloween night.

Right now, in this house, she was the closest she'd ever been to what she and my dad had always wanted. Worked for. Dreamed about.

I suddenly felt ungrateful and spoiled. If I couldn't be happy in the Playboy Mansion, well, then maybe I couldn't be happy anywhere. Maybe happiness wasn't a real thing. Maybe it was just a lie that we were all told, like Santa Claus and the Tooth Fairy.

Or maybe I was happy and I just didn't realize it.

"How about a tour," I said a little too brightly. "And I will tell you all about filming *The Girls Next Door*. It's so great!"

My mom visited fairly regularly after that. Every few months she would swoop in and fawn over Hef. The other girls seemed unsettled by her presence—probably wondering why someone's mom was there—but Hef adored her. She was bubbly and blond and fit right in. I always felt extra nervous when she visited, but Hef seemed okay with it. He called her pet names like "Goldie" or "Mama" and told her she could have been a Playmate in her day. I may have needed her in ways I couldn't fully articulate, but she so clearly basked in the glow of his attention and praise, I put my needs and fears aside.

I understood.

And the longer I stayed in the mansion, the easier it was to ignore the times I felt like I wanted to get out. I doubled down on making the best of it. I reminded myself of how badly I had wanted to get in here in the first place. I decided my anxiety wasn't actually about wanting to leave, but about making sure I could not only stay, but stay on top.

It helped that I was the main girlfriend, but it was by no means a permanent throne. Hef was temperamental, and there was no room for error. After a year, I still had barely carved out a place for myself at the mansion. Other than my clothes, there wouldn't have been a shred of evidence of my existence if I had been booted out tomorrow, not even a dent in the big master bed where I slept.

I'd be replaced within twenty-four hours, I was sure, by another woman with blonder hair, better breasts, and a better nose.

I had become obsessed with how bad my nose looked in the episodes we had filmed. I was more comfortable on camera than I had felt at the time of filming, but watching the show all I could focus on was the flaws in my face and my body.

If I wanted to stay, I needed to make myself flawless.

My first foray into plastic surgery had been the breast augmentation I got in college, when I was modeling and realized I needed a little more *oomph* in that department. My mom suggested the surgeon—it was someone who'd done some work for her before. That's how she phrased it: "getting a little something done" or "getting a little lift." She'd had several procedures by that point. The first one was when I was very young; my sisters hadn't yet moved out. We went to pick her up from the hospital, and when they brought her out in the wheelchair, we all burst into tears. Her whole head was wrapped in bandages, and what we could see of her face was bruised purple and green.

"I can hear you!" she'd mumbled at us through her teeth, which were bandaged shut.

We'd had to help her shower, my sisters holding her head and pouring water on her hair, careful not to get it on her incision. My oldest sister was the one to pull the staples out—one of the staples was bent the wrong way, so she had to twist it out while we all screamed.

For my new boobs, though, the surgeon had promised a different kind of experience, much cleaner and less traumatic. He was going to make a tiny incision in my belly button, then take these rolled up inserts, each like a silicone taquito, and slide them up under the skin of my abdomen, then position them under my breast tissue. Once in place, he would fill them with saline solution. He assured me it was all very safe, and better than the usual way of doing silicone implants because there would be no scarring whatsoever.

He didn't ask me what size I wanted, or really anything at all. I signed the forms, took the pre-surgery antibiotics; the day of the surgery, he drew on my bare torso with a special pen and then had me count down from one hundred. I passed out at ninety-eight and woke up in a stiff sports bra with newly inflated boobs. He was right; there were no incisions. I was so proud.

But after my mom drove me from the hospital to her place in San Diego, my abdomen began to burn, a searing pain worse than any menstrual cramp. I could barely sit up. The day after the surgery, when my mom and her housekeeper lifted me up to give me the pills I was prescribed, my blood pressure plummeted—low enough to kill someone—and I passed out. They called an ambulance to rush me back to the hospital, but after that, my memory blurs. It was traumatic, but it was worth it. It had to be.

My new breasts were tender and sore, but not too bad. The weird thing was that they pulled when I moved, like fabric snagging on something. It didn't feel right. When I asked about it, the doctor told me to do the recommended post-surgery exercises, which involved massaging the implants and doing arm stretches on both sides, so the implants didn't harden, but when I did, it was painful, and there were these ripping and popping noises. One of the implants was crooked, and didn't sit quite right against my rib cage. Something seemed off. But he assured me they just needed to settle.

Right off the bat, people noticed me more. I booked better jobs. And then of course, that night that I turned up at the mansion, I'd caught Hef's eye. I knew that never would have happened without those taquitos full of saline.

The plastic surgeon who did all of Hef's girls was "the one to go to for boobs." When I mentioned my hardened lump on one side of my breast, he examined me and told me that my immune system was reacting to the implant. Essentially, it was attacking it. My body was building scar tissue around the silicone shell, wrapping it in more and more layers, which were getting tighter and harder. He said he'd need to take it out, clean it off, and put it back in. Another doctor (the one to go to for noses) would do my nose at the same time.

I was relieved, because I could not see myself on screen or in a magazine photo or even in a mirror any longer without picking myself apart. And my nose was definitely an issue and, I believed, an obstacle to my happiness and my future.

The doctor asked me if I wanted to go ahead and do some liposuction while we were at it. He could suck the extra fat out of my hips, thighs, side, and butt for an extra four thousand.

I said yes to it all.

I woke up in a lipo girdle, a thick, tight-fitting, whole-body corset with a hole in the crotch so I could go to the bathroom. I could barely bend over. Everywhere was sore. I had two black eyes and a hardened gauze cone over my nose. They packed my nose with so much paper I could barely breathe, and my nose was like one of those paper towel dispensers where you pull the paper out of a hole in the bottom—which is exactly how it felt when I came back after recovering at the mansion for a few days and they pulled the paper out. It was like they were yanking out my brains.

When they took the gauze off my nose, I was shocked—it was so tiny. It looked like they'd taken my whole nose off. I kind of grabbed at it, confused, but the doctor assured me it would "puff back up," and sure enough, it did.

Years later, I would regret all of this: the surgery, the liposuction (turns out I needed that fat), the implants. But at the time, I had no idea how ill it would make me, that my body would reject the mold I was forcing it into.

All of the girlfriends had implants, nose jobs, and liposuction—there was simply no other way to be competitive.

It was unspoken but also very clear that there was no other option if I wanted to stay. And especially no other option if I wanted to get the one thing I was sure would catapult me to the next level.

I wanted nothing less than the holy grail of the *Playboy* world: centerfold.

I wanted it badly.

Every girl who came through those gates wanted to be a center-fold. It meant money, and fame, and opportunity. Centerfolds were their own subset of power within *Playboy*. They were paid for appearances separate from Hef, independent of Hef. They were a part of *Playboy* but also independent—it seemed like the best of both worlds to me. They became celebrities, famous actresses, and models. Centerfolds were a permanent part of *Playboy* history; once you became one it could never be taken away from you.

It was forever.

When the cameras starting rolling again for *The Girls Next Door*, my new nose and I got what I wanted: a *Playboy* pictorial. I was going to be Miss December 2009.

They filmed the magazine photo shoot for the show. It was exactly how I imagined a real photo shoot for *Playboy* magazine would be: very professional, high-level, respectful. I felt on top of my game. Assistants set up various scenes for me to pose in and described exactly how they wanted me to sit or stand. I loved getting a glimpse of the official, business side of *Playboy*—very different from sex toys in a cabinet and disposable cameras in the back of a limo.

The *Girls Next Door* producers had to get in some little drama, so at one point they directed my attention up, over my head, where someone had pinned a little green sprig.

"Uh oh," one of them said. "Is that . . . holly?"

In post-production, they added a little record-scratch sound right there, and zoomed in on my face. They were trying, as usual, to whip up some rivalry between me and Holly Madison.

Overall, though, I loved it. But then it was over.

My issue came out at Christmastime, and I flipped the magazine open to look at my pictorial. It looked good. I looked good. With the lighting and the touch-ups, in fact, I looked great. I'd done it—I'd made myself into a *Playboy* centerfold. I'd become one of those perfect, sexy creatures in a million copies of the magazine, all over the country. It was exciting, and I thought back to myself as a teenager and seeing those glossy magazines and the women in them for the first time. Could I ever have imagined I'd make it here? The answer was definitely no. I felt a tangle of emotions— I'd achieved something I was going for, but I felt sad, too. It was a weird blend of satisfaction and regret. The women on the cover of *Playboy* had seemed confident and powerful, and I thought I would feel the same way.

But at least this magazine cover was forever.

After filming ended, Mary finally suggested to the twins that they move out of the mansion and down the street into the Playmate House. It was the *Playboy* equivalent of a halfway house,

My dad, Ray Harris, and I in England. I'm two years old and smiling because I'm with my favorite person. Also, those curtains and chairs are amazing! *Courtesy of the author*

Greg and I at La Jolla High School. Same smile with another favorite person fourteen years later. *Courtesy of the author*

With Greg, at La Jolla High School— hanging with my love during lunch period. *Courtesy of the author*

At the Playboy Mansion on Halloween night, 2008. At the ropes, watching Hef in his cabana. Only minutes later, he would call me over and my life would change forever. © *HMH Foundation*

Halloween night, 2008, on the other side of the ropes. I felt special and chosen. I was twenty-one and he was eighty-one. © *HMH Foundation*

The Shannon twins sizing me up. © *HMH Foundation*

Awkward nights with girls I barely knew, upstairs in Hef's bedroom. Not everyone stayed when they knew what was to come. © *HMH Foundation*

Carl, the African crane, poolside at the mansion. He was a big grotto fan and wanted to be a Playmate. © *HMH Foundation*

One of the many peacocks around the mansion, in full display on Sunday Funday. © *HMH Foundation*

With my favorite boy, Charlie, in the pool. He was my most loyal friend at the mansion. © *HMH Foundation*

Amber and I in the pool during the summer of 2009. © *HMH Foundation*

Playmate of the Year trip to Vegas, wearing the bunny logo to represent. Hef called it "wearing the flag." © *HMH Foundation*

In the Hugh Hefner Suite at The Palms, Las Vegas. © *HMH Foundation*

Playboy limousines and jets and private security look impressive—but the logos were magnets, the plane was a loaner, and the security was made up of outsourced workers with bunny pins. © *HMH Foundation*

With Hef and my mom, whom he called Goldie. She was the only person I could tell that things at the mansion were not what they seemed. © *HMH Foundation*

Christmas at the mansion, but even the decorations looked weighed down by the drama. © *HMH Foundation*

Behind the scenes at the mansion was always a very different story than what the public saw. © *HMH Foundation*

Christmas with Hef and the Shannon twins. © *HMH Foundation*

Party at the mansion, my mom and Snoop Dogg kicking things off. © *HMH Foundation*

Another Halloween at the mansion, forced to smile even though I was not happy with a fake check-up by "All-the-Way Ray." © *HMH Foundation*

Movie night in 2016, when we were both getting sicker by the day in the mansion. © *HMH Foundation*

This is the face you make when you are suddenly engaged without a real proposal.
© *HMH Foundation*

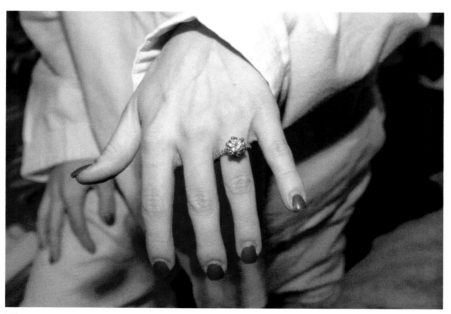

The engagement ring—my nails and I were both unprepared for this engagement.
© *HMH Foundation*

Looking out of the vanity with Hef. Usually this was my one place to be alone.
© *HMH Foundation*

Hef always knew when the camera was pointed at him, and relentlessly documented every occasion in his thousands of scrapbooks which are now in storage. © *HMH Foundation*

Wedding photo,
December 31, 2012.
© *HMH Foundation*

The wedding, 2012. My dress
was actually a pale pink, not
white, which was important to
me. © *HMH Foundation*

The wedding, 2012, with Charlie, my
best man, always. © *HMH Foundation*

Hef's birthday the year after we were married. © *HMH Foundation*

Hef's birthday cake, with our faces turned into Rick and Ilsa. © *HMH Foundation*

Twinning for yet another Halloween at the mansion. © *HMH Foundation*

 *from HUGH M. HEFNER*

DARLING—

I'M SCRAPBOOKING!

I LUV U!

Hef ♡

One of the many notes
that Hef left around
the house for me
during his last years.
© *HMH Foundation*

The back gate to the mansion, with the security house, in gray. Usually, these gates
were closed to keep people out...and in. © *HMH Foundation*

With Hef in the library in the later years and, of course, with backgammon. © *HMH Foundation*

Masquerade party at the mansion. Putting my new DJ skills to use. © *HMH Foundation*

Post-mansion life in 2021—the real me . . . © *Jack Guy*

but in this case it was for girls who were half-girlfriends, or half–pretty enough, or half in Hef's favor.

She transitioned them into the Playmate House, and not too long after that she transitioned them out of there and out of Hef's orbit altogether.

I felt relieved when they were permanently gone. I knew they were still teenagers, but they were never kind to me, and I constantly had to be looking over my shoulder when they were around. They also never stopped twinning, and like all twins who grow up and still go hard for twinning, it seemed like they were just one two-headed person.

I wasn't sorry to see them go, but I missed their help in the bedroom. Luckily Paige, a new Playmate who had moved into my old bedroom, was there to help me out, and Amber was always a phone call and a two-hour drive away when I needed her.

Paige was half in and half out like the twins, but more strategic about it. She moved into one of the bedrooms and collected her allowance, but many weekends she mysteriously had family she had to go visit. Family was always code for a boyfriend. Hef was more lenient with Paige and her weekend family visits, because she wasn't the main person in the room. I would never have gotten away with being gone on the weekends.

I could never get away.

It was the same with Holly, Bridget, and Kendra when they lived in the mansion. Kendra could always say she was going to San Diego to see her "family" and get away with it. I think that's why Holly resented Kendra.

Kendra had a secret life outside the mansion and could escape when she needed a break. The rest of us weren't so lucky.

Along with Paige, there were new girls who moved in and

out—one who stayed for a while hoarded lip gloss in a way that could only be a cry for help. There was another girl who looked just like a pinup girl from the 1920s. She was sexy, and voluptuous, and gorgeous. She desperately wanted to be a Playmate, and Hef made her dreams come true.

She was proud and excited, but in the middle of her excitement at seeing her own beautiful photos Hef got that glittery look in his eye.

"You know," he drawled, "you're the second heaviest Playmate after Anna Nicole Smith."

I watched as her face turned white, and she looked away from her photos. She laughed nervously, but I could see she was on the verge of tears.

"You are absolutely stunning," I said, and then I put my arm around her and asked if she wanted to go feed the monkeys.

Hef had a way of both boosting you up and cutting you down to size, often in the same conversation. I was getting used to being kept constantly on edge like this, constantly under threat. But I didn't like to see it when he did it to other women. Somehow I could be more outraged on their behalf than on my own.

After the twins were gone, it became my job to help find girls to come up to the bedroom at parties at the mansion, or on an increasingly rare night out. It was a big part of the reason we still went out at all: for Hef to find fresh girls.

Sometimes Hef would point someone out. Other times, I picked. He liked to have at least five girls, and I knew what he liked. It was actually a relief to have other women up in the bedroom with me, to not have to be sexual with him all alone. If these other girls were doing it, then I didn't have to. And there were always so many girls eager for a turn in Hugh Hefner's bed, sidling up to me at every party, desperate to be picked. I felt torn—part of me wanted to turn them down for their own good. But I also knew it was going to be someone coming up, so it might as well be someone who really wanted to go. I trusted that as adults they were making their own decisions about their bodies, but I also felt a responsibility to make the whole experience exciting for them. Or if not exciting then at least not so awkward.

Sometimes they would try to stick around, hanging on Hef and sucking up to him. There seemed to be an endless stream of women desperate to get into the mansion; it never slowed down. And it solidified the feeling even more that I couldn't possibly walk away. The more other people wanted what I had, the tighter I clung to it. When somebody stuck around for any length of time, I'd try to find out what they wanted. Girlfriend? Playmate? What?

It got to the point where I'd ask them, point blank. Surprised, they'd answer.

"Uh, Playmate," said one very young-looking girl named Talia.

Because I rarely left Hef's side, I was with him more often than not while he reviewed potential candidates for the pages of *Playboy*. I loved being over his shoulder, listening as he talked out loud about what worked in the magazine and what didn't. In those moments we felt like a team, and when he'd ask me what I thought, it seemed like he actually valued my opinion. Together we looked at thousands of pictures.

I could tell pretty quickly whether someone had the right look according to Hef, and was sure I knew whether it would be a yes or a no. I thought for sure Talia was going to be a no. Even so, I asked Mary in the office to send her for a test shoot. That way, the "no" would come from *Playboy*, not from me.

I happened to be in the hall when she popped out of her room and chased after Hef as he was just trying to get past her and into his office.

"I tested for *Playboy*!" she cried, excited.

"Mmm," he said, humoring her, but he made that face he always made when he was trying to escape someone who did not interest him: a tight, closed-mouth smile.

She pursued him, babbling about the shoot and how well it had gone. He didn't respond, moving to close his office door. Desperately, she stepped closer.

"So what do you think about that?" she asked, looking at him hopefully.

"Well, we'll see what the pictures look like," he said, "but it's probably going to be a no."

And he shut the door in her face.

I brought Talia into the big black marble bathroom and handed her a tissue to wipe away her tears. "You'll be okay," I said.

She started to cry even louder.

"It's for the best, really," I said, just a little too sharply. In this moment, she wasn't competition; she was a mirror.

I couldn't say what I wanted to say to her. I couldn't tell her living here wasn't like what she imagined. I was still distrustful of other women, and on guard, but I had compassion for her. "Go back home," I said. "Maybe you could go to college, or take acting classes, or maybe there's something you love to do that you don't even know about yet. You're free to do whatever you want; that's amazing!"

She looked at me like I was crazy. She looked at me like I was the last person she could trust for advice.

"I'm going to keep trying," she said. "I am not going to give up, ever." And then she turned and walked out.

I walked over to the empty birdcage that hung in the corner of the bathroom. When I first got there it had had two lovebirds in it. They were small and bright green, with the sweetest little rosy cheeks. I loved how pretty they were, and that they supposedly had a very strong pair bond, where they would fall in love and be loyal to each other. The problem was, they kept dying. Every time one of them turned up dead on the cage floor, lying there as still as a little green banana, the staff would whisk it away and replace it with a new, live bird. The new pair would have to rebond with each other, now that the previous partner was gone. But then another one would die.

Nobody had any idea what was going on, and finally, they stopped replacing the birds. I finally went and looked the cage over, searching for some reason they were dying other than the fact there was no sunlight in the bathroom at all.

Maybe something had been overlooked because of how fast the staff had to clean when they came into Hef's room—he was turning into something of a hoarder, with stacks of papers and files and photos and books building up all over the bedroom, to the point that the sunlight coming in the windows would bleach the carpet all around the stacks, leaving a bright square of fresh red underneath. The staff was overwhelmed, and it was all they could do to dust and vacuum and keep things down to a dull roar. The birds got overlooked.

It turned out there was something wrong with the watering device, a bottle with a little metal straw. There was a metal pea at the end of the straw that allowed the water to flow out when a bird pecked it. But it had gotten stuck. The thing wouldn't dispense water. That was it—such an easy thing to fix, but nobody noticed. The birds had been dying of thirst this whole time, and the mansion staff just kept replacing them, bird after bird.

CHAPTER 10

Stick to the Schedule

Mondays were for the men. Hef called it Manly Monday.

Every week a group of Hef's friends joined him for movie night, men only, no women allowed. They gathered together for dinner, discussion, and a movie. Hef didn't join them for dinner, instead choosing to eat in his bedroom. He never joined the buffet downstairs, preferring to eat the same pre-movie food on a tray in his bedroom—canned chicken noodle soup, saltines, and a block of cream cheese. Later he would have his regular dinner of pork chops and mashed potatoes if he was still hungry, or if it was a sex night, he would have a BLT sandwich.

Every night was movie night, but Mondays were for Hef's acolytes—a group of long-standing friends, his brother Keith, Ray Anthony, Richard Bann, Kevin Burns, and others in his inner circle. They would bring articles that featured Hef, and they all would read and discuss and feed and flatter his ego. He was keenly interested in any bit of media that talked about him, and bored by anything in print that wasn't about him. He knew about politics and could opine when it counted, but in truth any news that wasn't Hef news was dismissed as irrelevant. Three Mondays a month they would talk about old movies—*12 Angry Men, The Maltese Falcon, Some Like It Hot, On the Waterfront, Citizen Kane*— the list was endless. Then they would vote on which movie to watch after each person discussed why they chose that particular film. They discussed the actors endlessly and dissected everything about them, even more than the plots or themes in the movie.

One Monday a month they dissected women. Hef would use that Monday to pass around the latest issue of *Playboy,* and the men would peruse the magazine like a *Playbill* and discuss the merits of each body part of the women featured. These men, all over the age of fifty, reviewed, they passed judgment, and they voted. Satisfied with themselves after combing the latest issue, they settled in to watch a movie. Sometimes I fantasized about gathering a group of women together and passing around a photo of a naked man so we could pass judgment, so we could point out all their flaws. It was just a fantasy, though, because that would never have happened.

But more and more my mind entertained these innocent but subversive thoughts, while the rest of me went along with the program.

I loved Mondays. It meant my curfew was nine-thirty p.m. and not the usual six p.m. Sometimes I went to Mary's house to play cards on Mondays, but only because it was a good thing to do politically. It still felt like being in the mansion, and I didn't want to waste my one late curfew. Whenever I complained about my curfew, the staff would always say, "Nothing good happens after nine-thirty p.m. anyway."

In their way they were trying to comfort me, but being controlled never feels comfortable.

Tuesday was game night—dominos and Uno—girls and Hef only. I was in charge of picking the girls on that night, so I tried to pick ones who weren't desperate to move into the mansion. Girls who wouldn't be a threat to me. I always brought Amber and Hef's brother's wife, or a married Playmate. I filled it in with girls who either weren't Hef's type or whom I considered friends. The games dragged on for hours, and sometimes Hef would nod off. I knew it was because of all the pain meds—Percocet—he was taking. But Hef's opiate addiction was a secret from the rest of the world. It had started because of his back pain, originally, legitimately. But Hef's addiction to pills was a well-known secret in the house, and one nobody ever talked about.

Supposedly, when Hef first started the magazine, he was addicted to Dexedrine—a speedy drug popular back in the seventies. Or maybe it was just speed. He'd stay up all night working on the magazine, and then there were the Quaaludes. He also smoked his famous pipe for years and years until he had a stroke. He called it "a stroke of luck" since it made him give up the pipe. But then came the Percocet. Doctors had no problem prescribing him opiates—he was a celebrity—and his doctors had given him an "earthquake supply" of Percocet. We didn't know until much later just how much he had tapped into that earthquake supply in addition to his regular monthly refills.

His hearing was also shot, which made Uno the better game to play because we yelled that out anyway. There was research that suggested taking copious amounts of Viagra caused hearing loss, but Hef would give up a limb before he gave that up. The truth was he was an older man trying to keep up with his own lifestyle—and some days it was easier for him than others. But it was one more thing we could never talk about.

Wednesday was the same Monday night man crew but for gin rummy. They invited men outside their inner circle that night, but I never knew their criteria for the guests. It could be someone in the news, or an actor, or maybe just someone who was good at cards. My curfew was also later, eight-thirty p.m., on Wednesdays. It wasn't quite as nice as Mondays, but I could still breathe a little.

Thursdays were for going out on the town, at least in the beginning. Later they became another movie night, but I was allowed to pick the movie. I picked movies that I knew would piss the guests off who had come for a hopefully decadent Playboy Mansion experience. I'd choose *The Little Mermaid* or any movie that wasn't sexy at all, just because I could. I was powerful on Thursday movie night, until halfway through the movie I'd see Hef pull out a little tissue and unwrap a small blue pill. My stomach would flip. I knew that meant I'd have to bring women up to the bedroom and perform. During the second half of the movie it was almost like I could smell the baby oil, and I would feel nauseous.

Friday and Saturday were Casablanca nights. Once a year Hef would go into the attic at the mansion and pick classic movies to play for the entire year. These movies would play on Casablanca nights, and Hef would stand up before the crowd of twenty or so people at the mansion for movie night and read his notes for a particular movie—why he chose it, why it mattered, what he liked about it, where it fit in history. He was a movie critic, a movie connoisseur, and these old timey films were his jam.

When he was done pontificating, he'd wave his arm with a flourish at the projector guys, and yell, "It's movie time!" Then an old cartoon would play first, because that's how they did it in his day, and then the movie.

In these old movies, a woman was always being saved by one man from another man. Or they were completely passive, except for when they were flirting with a man or trying to lead him into temptation. They were silly, weak, or dumb, and everything in their life revolved around getting the man. They fawned or fainted. They couldn't make decisions for themselves. Sometimes I would turn my head and watch Hef watching them. No matter how many times he had seen the same movie, he was enraptured by the stereotypical roles on the screen.

I may have dropped out of school before I finished my psychology degree, but I could recognize projection and psychodrama when it was in front of me.

Sundays we were back to the false fun in the sun—roller-skating, hula hoops, trampolines, and lollipops—then another movie, usually whatever was currently playing in theaters. If it rained on Sundays we would all cram into the game house and fake our girly fun in close quarters while the men watched from their backgammon games on one side of the room. No bathing suits indoors, but the outfits still had to be sexy, and it was cramped and miserable.

On Mondays it would start all over again. Lather. Rinse. Repeat.

I didn't feel panic on Sundays anymore, but I did feel something close to anger. I had never been an angry person, and whenever I got really mad it usually came out as tears, which was frustrating. But there was something in me that wanted to rebel at it all. I was annoyed, irritated. Day after day, week after week, year after year now, it was the same exact thing.

This was the life I had chosen, the life I thought I wanted. But I was bored out of my mind. As much as the world of *Playboy* represented freedom and excess, I mostly felt restricted. I missed spontaneity. I had longed to be taken care of, to have someone, anyone, make decisions for me, to be in a safe place. But the downside of living in a safe and controlled environment is that you have no control.

I didn't recognize it right away. I wish I had. I wish I had seen all the ways I was being exactly like those women in the classic movies I judged. I wish I had been able to resist the constant wearing down of my self-esteem, my free will. But hindsight is everything, and at the time I was too young and too new to the world to express all the ways the *Playboy* world rubbed my skin the wrong way: the ways it chafed my joy, my peace, my very soul.

Sometimes knowing how every single day is going to be feels better than stepping into the unknown. I was still competing every day in a race I had voluntarily signed up for, and I had absolutely no idea that I could simply step off the track. Hef constantly reminded me how lucky I was to be there. How fortunate.

One time I mentioned wanting to give my old car, a car Hef had given me, to my mom. I expected he would smile and nod, because old cars were always passed on so they didn't take up space at the mansion. But he didn't. He snapped at me. "I'm not here to support your family."

I instantly felt ashamed; I wasn't asking for a handout, just that it go to my mom instead of charity. He had subtle ways of reminding me that my position was precarious.

"It's so lucky for you that you live here," he'd say randomly out of nowhere.

At parties sometimes he'd come in for one of his classic open-mouthed kisses, and then whisper in my ear, "There are so many beautiful women here." Then a little bit later he'd do it again, only this time he'd say, "It's unfortunate that the majority of the population is unattractive, especially women."

Then he'd look me up and down and shrug. He did it to keep me on edge, and it worked.

So, yes, I hated every single rigid day of the week, but I especially hated Friday mornings.

Allowance day.

My first time getting allowance was with the twins—I think they wanted to keep it from me for as long as possible—but a couple of weeks after I moved in, I overheard them talking about "getting our allowance from Hef."

I edged into the hallway where they were standing.

"What do you mean, allowance?" I asked.

Grudgingly, they explained: On Fridays we each got an allowance, which we were expected to spend on clothes and whatever other beauty maintenance or accessories we needed in order to present as *Playboy* girlfriends. Within those general expectations, we got to decide how to spend it. But we had to go and ask for it.

When they headed down the hallway toward Hef's bedroom, I followed. I felt like a loser trailing after these girls who disliked me and clearly didn't want me around, but I reminded myself that I was a girlfriend now just like them, so whatever they were getting, I should get, too.

Hef wasn't surprised to see the three of us turn up—he seemed smug and expectant. Karissa and Kristina immediately turned on the charm. They were dressed, as usual, in matching outfits: tiny velour sport shorts and tank tops that showed off their perfectly tanned breasts. I was starting to feel self-conscious about my own—this was before my mansion plastic surgery. I was still self-conscious and insecure in general about being in the mansion. The twins, meanwhile, posed and cocked their hips, smiling flirtatiously at him.

"Can we have our allowance, please, Hef?" they cooed in unison, in a sing-song girly tone. They sounded like teenage daughters asking their father for spending money, but in fairness they were only nineteen, so they *were* teenagers.

It was obvious that the asking was yet another performance to please Hef and to remind us of our dependence on his generosity.

Hef played his part, the benevolent benefactor. It was obvious that he enjoyed it, that he relished being asked, and wanted to linger in this moment where he had the upper hand.

"Of course, of course," he said, with fake surprise, as though he needed to be reminded.

Theatrically, he pulled out a velvet pouch. From that, he produced a key. He unlocked his special cabinet—the one that held his fancy, inlaid wooden box full of marijuana and pills. The cabinet that held the sex toys. And now I could see it was also the cabinet that held an envelope stuffed full of cash: fresh, crisp one-hundred-dollar bills. Later I would discover that Norma, one of the office ladies, restocked the envelope of cash every week, so that he could perform this ritual with his girlfriends.

He began counting out the bills into three stacks, slowly and deliberately: *one...two...three...*all the way to ten. One thousand dollars each.

I stood there for what felt like a long time while he counted out the money. He seemed to take a long time on purpose, laying down each bill, neatening the stacks. He made us wait. And wait we did, hands clasped like good girls. I felt terrible. I felt like a hooker. Hot shame rose inside me, my cheeks burning; I realized my face was turning bright red. A little voice inside me whispered, *What are you doing?*

I pushed the voice away. And when he held out the stack of bills to me, I took it.

The ritual continued after the twins left, of course: Every Friday I, and whoever was living in the other bedrooms, had to go ask for our allowance. It was demoralizing on purpose. It was infantile. But since we couldn't work outside the house, it was our only source of income.

Sometimes I imagined throwing the money back at him. "I don't need your money," I would say coldly, and then I would walk away.

But I did need it. If I didn't have any cash I wouldn't have gas money, and I'd never be able to leave the house. Hef was careful not to give us too much money, and he watched to make sure that we spent it on what we were supposed to be spending it on. He didn't want us building any kind of nest egg.

My fantasy that somehow Hef and I would develop a real relationship was over not long after our season of *The Girls Next Door* premiered. This wasn't a relationship, it was a job, and as soon as I accepted that reality my panicky feelings began to lessen. My job was to perform. I performed on his television show, for Hef's friends and guests, and for him, in his bedroom.

The sex never changed, only the faces: The silk pajamas. The four big television screens with the same old porn reels playing. Hef getting into bed and reaching for the baby oil. We were all getting infections from the baby oil—it wasn't supposed to be used as lube. I tried to tell him, I begged Mary to tell him, but you couldn't really tell him anything he didn't want to hear. We tried to replace the baby oil with lube, but when we weren't looking, he would always switch it back.

He kept a doctor on retainer who would come when called to give us antibiotics.

To avoid infections, I sometimes resorted to anal sex when it was my turn to straddle Hef. I don't think he could ever tell the difference, and it helped me avoid a host of frontal issues. It wasn't always the easiest, but it was the best solution I could think of.

The sex had become like everything at the mansion—part of my job.

I knew by then exactly what he liked—how he wanted me to move, what I should sound like and look like—and so I did it. Sometimes, though, I was shocked that he actually fell for it. How could he not see that for all of us it was an act? Did he really think we were enjoying it? Somehow, he actually *did*. I found myself wondering: Did he just assume that this was what everyone liked, because it's what he liked? Or was he just this self-obsessed? Or maybe he just didn't care. He seemed less sex-savvy than some of the teenage boys I'd been with years ago, when I was just figuring out how to have fun with my sexuality, how to please someone else and help them to please me, too. It was clear to me that Hef had never taken a moment in his entire life to figure out how to please someone else.

Even the first time, the sex hadn't exactly been fun. But there'd been a thrill to it, a sense of possibility, of doing something wild, something unusual. It felt young and sexy and free. The Playboy Mansion had a reputation, a legacy as one of the first sex-positive, liberated places. Now, I wondered if that place had ever really existed. Hef's public persona, the narrative that everyone bought into, was of a powerful man who used that power to elevate women, fight for civil rights, and champion the First Amendment. He was the poster boy for sexual liberation. I never felt very liberated in his bedroom. He always framed it as a choice—but of course he also reminded you that the opportunity was in the staying. But the longer you stayed, the more hoops you jumped through and the more you were programmed to believe that you would be nothing if you left.

It was an invisible trap framed by the language of choice.

I didn't believe in the happily-ever-after I had once imagined in Monaco, but the idea that I'd made a mistake terrified me. I'd invested far too much already. I had come too far from Owen in San Diego to go back to that life. I didn't want to be the ex–main girlfriend of Hugh Hefner handing out t-shirts at monster truck rallies.

I didn't know what I wanted to be or do when I grew up, so this modern day harem that I'd joined—that I was the leader of—was my best option.

In college I'd learned about the "sunk cost fallacy," which is when someone is so heavily invested in something, they don't walk away, even if it would be better for them if they did. A gambler who's lost thousands will bet their last hundred on one last round and lose it, instead of escaping with that last little bit. A real estate investor keeps pouring more money into a bad deal instead of accepting the initial loss. I was deep in the throes of sunk cost fallacy. I'd invested so much that I couldn't just walk away.

And for all Hef's power, I thought that he needed me. He didn't know, wouldn't admit that he needed me in any real way, but I wasn't someone who was going to steal from him or trick him or humiliate him in public. In many ways, I was the perfect person for the job.

On the little blue pill nights, to make it easier, I made sure we always played the same CD—the Madonna track he had played the first night I stayed over. He liked to have music on, and he preferred this one because it was boppy and upbeat; it jibed with his idea that we were all having a fun party time. It made a strange, surreal soundtrack for what we were doing, but I'd put it on just the same, and forward to the same track every time.

Gonna dress you up in my love, all over, all over—

The song played on repeat, over and over again. I didn't want any other music on while we had sex, ever. I didn't want to associate any other songs, especially ones I actually liked, with this room. I knew that, later, I would not want to remember these years. I didn't want to one day be wandering through a supermarket and suddenly hear a song that dragged me back to this time. So I calculated: *If I just play this one song always, then no other music will be contaminated by this place.* If I made sure that this was the only song that reminded me of these moments, then the easier it would be, later, to contain these memories, lock them up in a box, and bury them deep.

Sometimes sex is just sex; fun, easy, no big deal. But when sex gets combined with power and control, when you can't say no to it easily or without repercussions to your sense of security, it takes on a different tenor. I knew that one day if I was ever in a real relationship, where sex was about pleasure and intimacy and actual lovemaking, I would regret these nights in the bedroom. I would regret the ways I compromised and betrayed myself.

But most nights I just did my job, and on the rare occasion when I could faintly hear a little voice inside me whispering *this isn't good for us*, I just turned the music up louder.

CHAPTER 11

Prey

As Season 6 of *The Girls Next Door* was premiering, *Playboy* threw me onto talk shows right away to promote the show. I was given no instructions, no prep, no media training. As long as my hair, makeup, and clothes were flawless and screamed "*Playboy* girlfriend," that seemed to be all anyone cared about. Sometimes Hef would look me over before an appearance and send me back to my room to change into something brighter or sexier. "Wear the flag," he'd say, which meant to put on something with a *Playboy* bunny logo on it.

Every media appearance sent me into a cold panic. I walked into them believing that if I was myself—if I was kind and answered each question honestly and politely—the interview would go great. The questions were never very kind. The hosts asked the invasive, personal questions right off the bat. *What's it like to have sex with an old guy? Are old balls gross? Do you get it on with other girls? Were you always a gold digger?* They'd go right to their fantasies about me, to the things that horrified, thrilled, or disgusted them. I could tell they thought I was sex crazed or a sex worker or sexually deviant in some mysterious way. It was unfair and wrong, but what was even worse was that I could also tell they thought I was stupid and shallow.

I wasn't human. I was a punch line.

They thought as a talk show guest I was an easy kill.

And they were right.

I made the radio show rounds and appeared on some entertainment news shows. When the producers booked me on Chelsea Handler's show I had high hopes for the interview—I knew she was funny, and she was a woman fighting her way to the top in an industry dominated by men. I thought maybe she'd be more compassionate. I thought we might have a real conversation. I thought as a female comedian she'd be more evolved than her male counterparts. But she went right for the jugular, too.

"What does your dad think?" she asked me as I sweated under the stage lights, trying to keep a smile on my face.

"Oh," I said. "He passed away."

She turned to the audience with a big grin.

"Well, there you have it, folks," she announced. "Daddy issues!"

The crowd burst out laughing. I sat in silence as the pain of her words washed over me.

I did have daddy issues, whatever that means. I was instantly transported to the trauma of his death. I was on a talk show, but I was twelve years old and losing my father. I was twelve years old and without a home to call my own. As the studio audience laughed and Chelsea Handler grinned at her own cleverness, I smiled and smiled and laughed along with everybody else at my expense.

It felt like I was floating outside my own body.

Terri Thomerson, the *Playboy* publicist, could tell I was distraught after I left the stage. "I'll say something to the producers," she said, "to see if they can take that portion out." The producers agreed—even to them, it seemed like too much. But the damage had been done.

I didn't know how to answer crass questions designed to exploit me. Every interviewer felt like a circling shark as I struggled to tread in deep water. I babbled nervously whenever the conversation seemed to lag, and I said too much. I knew I needed help to navigate these interviews. And it became clear that I wasn't going to get that help at the mansion, so I hired a woman in Los Angeles for an intensive three-day media training session. It cost me two weeks of allowance, but I was willing to pay anything I had to never feel like I felt with Chelsea Handler.

I learned that I didn't need to fill awkward gaps in the conversation—that was on the interviewer. It sounded simple, but it was revolutionary. The idea that it wasn't up to me to make sure the interviews went well blew my mind. I was so used to people pleasing and making sure everyone around me had what they needed from me, and that made this new boundary not only strange but almost uncomfortable. The media trainer told me that I could say "no," and I looked at her as if she had sprouted antennae out of the top of her head.

I may not have always had the best boundaries when it came to relationships, but after my time in the mansion I was so automatically compliant and timid, the ability to say the word "no" shook me. Hearing her tell me I didn't have to answer a question if I didn't want to felt like the most empowering thing I had ever heard.

It felt nothing short of revolutionary.

And I wondered why Hef or *Playboy* or even the television show producers hadn't thought to prepare me.

But even after the training, the feeling of being hunted never went away. I was an easy target for journalists, and they went in for the kill every single time. My body was up for comment. My sexuality. My morality. My personality and my intelligence were disrespected and disregarded. The media became yet another place where I was supposed to smile and play nice, even while those around me played dirty.

I thought my association with *Playboy* would finally make me feel worthy. I thought the high school years of feeling like I wasn't enough because I didn't have the right clothes or the right hair color or the right address were behind me. I had no idea that it would feel worse than high school bullying, because these were grown men and women who judged me for my clothing and my hair color and my *Playboy* address.

There are so many ways to dehumanize a person. Dismiss them. Laugh at their expense. Take advantage of them.

Even with the new training, I was still years away from knowing that how the talk show hosts, journalists, and shock-jock DJs treated me said more about who they were than who I was. I may have had a new nose, better breasts, and a smoother body, but even that external armor was no match for the people in the media who only saw it as a reason to attack who I was on the inside.

And it wasn't just the media who saw me as prey, because as soon as the show aired and the publicity started—the men came out to get their piece of the kill.

An older guy I had once dated before the mansion called and offered me the use of his house in Redondo Beach if I ever needed to get away from it all. In truth, I needed to get away from it all every single day until curfew, but I knew not to say that out loud to anyone. So I made the forty-five-minute drive to Redondo and spent the day by myself in his home. In the mansion I could never just lounge around in bed—if I wasn't fawning over Hef and playacting my role as girlfriend, I had to be vigilant of the staff who continued to spy on me.

Everything was transactional, and even after two years the feeling of being hunted never left me, so I took my respite in Redondo when I could. Until the guy I used to date, who so generously lent me his house as a sanctuary, decided to blackmail me. He called the mansion and told them I was meeting lovers at his house. He said he would go public with the information.

They paid him to go away.

It didn't matter if it was true or not, or how I felt used and exploited. Going public would have been an embarrassment for the man that was Hugh Hefner: the man who was so sexually satisfying no woman would ever want another man in her bed.

That man I once dated was the first man to blackmail me, but he wouldn't be the last. Over the years I would be set up again, falling for con men like the one from *The Bachelor* show who met me under the guise of selling wine to the mansion and manipulated me into confiding that I felt trapped and unhappy. "It kind of sucks," I had said honestly.

I didn't know he was secretly recording me.

Hef paid him $15,000 to destroy the audio recording of me admitting my unhappiness. At no time did anyone step up and tell me that blackmail is illegal. Secretly recording someone is illegal. Nobody, not Hef, not Mary, not the *Playboy* lawyers, ever asked if what was on the recording was true—if I was unhappy. They didn't care that I thought life at the mansion kind of sucked; they only cared that I had said it out loud.

I couldn't trust anyone in the mansion, and then I couldn't trust anyone outside of the mansion. I felt exposed and vulnerable, and more alone than ever.

And the mansion still seemed like the safest place for me to be.

CHAPTER 12

America's Princess

On Christmas Eve 2010, Hef handed me a little music box. It had mermaids in a seascape painted on the outside of it, and when I opened the lid, a tiny Ariel from *The Little Mermaid* rose up and twirled. "Part of Your World" began to play, in those twinkly metallic music box notes.

He knew I loved *The Little Mermaid*—I'd watched it dozens of times as a kid, and probably dozens more since I'd been in the mansion. I loved the story of the mermaid princess who wants so badly to belong to a different, sunnier world, she trades her voice for a chance to walk around on human legs and find love. I was touched by the uncharacteristically thoughtful gift from Hef.

Then I noticed it. Next to Ariel, on the velvet lining, there was a ring.

An engagement ring.

"I hope it fits," was all Hef said.

As far as romantic proposals go, it wasn't. We hadn't even talked about marriage, we weren't in love, and I was confused. I blinked and looked around the room.

"But..."

Hef interrupted me. "It should fit. Mary helped me with the size."

I got the message loud and clear, so I picked up the ring and slipped it on in front of everyone there: the other girlfriends, some Playmates, the staff, a photographer, and several cameramen filming for *The Girls Next Door*. It was Christmas at the mansion, after all—always a big production. I didn't know why the cameramen for the show were there; we weren't shooting another season.

The ring fit. Everyone clapped. Cameras flashed.

Hef never actually asked me to marry him. I never said yes.

I tried to talk about marriage as we went to sleep, but Hef made it clear there was nothing more to say on the subject and went right to sleep. I lay awake staring up at the ceiling mirror. *Engaged? He wanted to marry me?* I didn't know how to feel or what it meant. I didn't feel excited. I didn't feel worried. It felt like another pretend scenario—like when we were filming and pretended we wanted to sleep in a tent in the yard. I felt remarkably numb. Curious, but numb.

A press release had already gone out by the time I woke up, one that had been prepared days before. I still hadn't said yes, but from that moment, we were engaged, and the *Playboy* machine whirred toward its next big publicity event: a grand wedding.

Right away, they started planning a TV special called *Marrying Hef*, a reality series featuring me. I realized this had all been planned earlier as well, and that was why the cameras were in place to capture the engagement. The show was going to follow me around with cameras for months, capturing everything about the wedding, from picking out a dress to tasting cakes to choosing flowers and planning seating charts.

Hef sensed my uncertainty, my hesitation, and definitely my bewilderment at how fast this was happening and how much had already been planned without me knowing. Just as no one asked me if I wanted to get married, no one asked me if I wanted to do an entire show about a wedding I hadn't agreed to.

"I have a surprise for you," he said one day shortly after our engagement.

"What?" I was afraid to really hear the answer, but the cameras had already starting rolling for the wedding show, so I smiled big and tried to look enthusiastic.

"You're going to like this," he said. "How would you like to be on the cover, Mrs. Hefner?"

The cover was what every girl in the house, and every Playmate who had ever been featured on the inside of the magazine coveted. I should have been jumping for joy. But I still felt oddly numb.

Partly, I was a bit blindsided that Hef wanted this—I hadn't seen it coming. Marriage to the legendary Hugh Hefner . . . I knew it was supposed to be this big win. According to Mary, Holly had always been pushing for it over the seven years she spent as the main girlfriend at the mansion. It seemed like the ultimate prize. But what was this? I couldn't seem to wrap my mind around it, and I didn't like that it had all been planned as if I had no say in the matter. But I wasn't really too surprised at it, either.

I still wasn't sure if it was a real proposal for a real marriage, or just something for the show, and Hef didn't seem like he wanted to talk about it except in front of the cameras.

I felt too young to get married. And if I were to make a list of what I wanted in a husband, Hef wouldn't be it, unless my list included power hungry and lonely, with a deep need to control everything and everyone around him. He was a narcissist. He only ever thought of himself. At his last birthday, one of his famous guests had given him a beautiful bound book of *New York Times* articles printed on his birthdate through the years. After the party, he flipped the book open to peruse it. As soon as he saw that there were no articles about him personally, he stood up and threw the book in the trash.

He was deeply insecure and made up for it by surrounding himself with people who would fawn over him and make him feel adored. He was a person—like a lot of people—who still carried childhood wounds. I knew he never felt loved as a child; I knew about his first crush who went on a hayride with another boy, about the woman he left to go off to war, who cheated on him while he was gone. I knew about these things not because we actually talked about them, but because they had been written about him by others in books and magazine articles and newspaper features, and then he read those articles about himself and repeated the stories. He never said more than what was written. He never expressed any emotional range beyond saying he was sad. Sometimes he would stick out his lower lip to emphasize that he was extra sad, but the only time I saw him close to genuinely feeling an emotion like sadness was when he was watching *Casablanca*.

It never occurred to him to be curious about other people, unless it was for the show or in a media interview. He barely even seemed interested in his own children. I didn't think he knew *how* to love.

None of these were qualities I wanted in my future husband. None of these were things I dreamed of when I dreamed of whom I would marry. Hef was not a Disney prince. But of course, I wasn't a Disney princess, either. And life in the mansion wasn't the fairy tale I had once hoped it would be. From the outside, sure, it had all the trappings of a fairy tale. But it wasn't, and anyone who lived there knew it.

The other haunting fact that overshadowed everything when

thinking about Hef as a husband was that he knew that he could draw in vulnerable women like a magnet and have them do whatever he wanted in exchange for even the *possibility* of a payoff: status, some money, a modeling job. But the worst part about it was the way it was never made explicit. You went into his orbit offering all of yourself—and you had no idea what you'd get back, if anything. He *might* hand you an allowance, or some "gas money" as he called it, for the girls who stopped in, or he might not. He might pass your pictures on to the *Playboy* editors, or he might give them the thumbs down. Maybe your proximity to him would get you somewhere. But maybe you'd walk out of there with nothing, after making a bad trade where you got the losing end. It was all according to his whim. And he knew it.

He reveled in it.

Power is insidious when it masks itself as generosity. And generosity is insidious when it's a camouflage for control. And both power and generosity are confusing when they gaslight you into believing they could be love.

I didn't know whether to be sad for Hef or angry. He was so desperate for love and adoration, but he had no clue how to give it to anyone else. All he knew how to do was manipulate and leverage his power. I felt like a pawn. What did he even want me for? Why was this ring on my finger? I felt like an object in this house, a *thing*, like a carved statue or a painting hanging on the wall. Something to be used, looked at, enjoyed. When would I get to be a person?

I was simply another experiment in his weird Frankenstein fascination. The memorabilia I thought was just for Halloween that first night I entered the house was a permanent fixture and permeated the entire house. Dr. Frankenstein thought he was building the perfect creature—mixing body parts and bringing a man to life. Playing God. Hef would never willingly look too deeply at the psychology behind his Frankenstein obsession—one he shared with the producer of *The Girls Next Door*. Or maybe they both knew what it meant. Maybe it was an inside joke. We weren't women, just interchangeable body parts manipulated to fulfill the fantasies of a man's twisted mind. Built to feed one man's hubris.

And then sell that man's fantasies to the entire world.

So my heart didn't soar when a man who couldn't love put a ring on my finger. The cameras flashed, and the acolytes cheered, and I smiled the way I had been taught. But he never asked me if I wanted to marry him, and I never answered, because it wasn't a question. It wasn't a choice.

Like all things with Hef, it was a transaction—cover of *Playboy* equaled marriage and marriage equaled the cover of *Playboy*.

I would go along with it because going along with things was what I did.

That was my job.

We did the photo shoot for the *Playboy* cover soon after. They dressed me in some of Hef's signature items: the dark red robe, a white captain's hat with the black trim. Robe thrown open, I wore a black lace bra on top and nothing else. The headline was going to read, "America's Princess: Introducing Mrs. Crystal Hefner."

The publicist started taking me around to flower shops, cake tastings, dress fittings. A camera crew followed, filming everything. In the middle of it all, Hef came to me while I was sitting in the vanity and dropped some papers in my lap to sign. As I flipped through, I saw that it was a contract for the show *Marrying Hef*. After getting nothing for *The Girls Next Door*, I had a tiny leap of hope, that maybe he did respect me enough to pay me for my work. My heart sunk when I saw what he was giving me: a token $2,500 "talent fee" for the whole series. I had overheard Hef and the producer, Kevin, talking excitedly about what their earnings from the marriage show were going to be—$800,000. My fee was like pennies compared to that, and I was the one filming every day.

I was furious.

I tried to keep my voice steady as I told him that I'd overheard him and Kevin talking about how much money they were making for the show. How much they were making off of *me*. "I'm not expecting half or anything, of course not," I added quickly. "But...maybe something more significant than this?" *Something to make me feel valued*, I thought but didn't say. *Like I have a seat at the table.*

Hef studied me, eyebrows raised.

"What are you in this for?" he asked coolly. It felt like an accusation—as if I was a gold digger, like everyone else assumed, like in those media interviews I had been forced to do.

And in that moment, I snapped. I realized that *Playboy* was going to squeeze everything they could out of me for as long as I stayed here. Hef and this whole organization were going to juice me like a lemon. There was never going to be an upside.

I stormed out of the vanity, brushing past him and slamming the bedroom door. I ran down the stairs and stalked out of the mansion, shaking. I was shaking because I was furious. I was shaking because I had never had an outburst like that before in the mansion, never shown anger and certainly not rage. I had never fought back on anything with him, never questioned or contradicted him. It was exhilarating and also terrifying. No one slammed a door on Hugh Hefner.

But I did.

I had nothing with me. All of my belongings were still in the house—everything I owned in the world. But I didn't care. I had to get out, off this property, *away*, as fast as humanly possible. I stormed down the driveway toward the security gate. I started running.

Then I heard his voice over the mansion loudspeaker.

"Close the back gate!" he boomed. "If Crystal tries to leave, detain her!"

I stopped. My whole body went cold.

I had spent so much time trying to decide whether to leave or stay that I never considered, even with the curfews and the rigid schedules and the sex where consent was a given, that it wasn't my choice. I thought I was a figurative prisoner, locked into this house because of my own fear of not being able to build a life on my own, because I had been programmed to believe that the minute I stepped away from Hef, from his world, I was nothing. I never thought I was an actual prisoner.

Detain her.

I stood there frozen. I could see security below me, the men with grim looks on their faces. They weren't bad guys—but they were Hef's guys. They did as they were told, because they needed the income. They liked me, sure, but not enough to lose their jobs over me. They had barricaded me in, and my mind never went to what would have happened if I tried to get out. Would they have physically restrained me? Would Hef lock me into a tower in his castle? Had I gone from a sad Cinderella wanting to get into the ball to a prisoner in the dungeon who couldn't get out?

The sky was turning dark. The peacocks were moving over the lawn toward their roost, dragging their long tails, which swished softly over the grass like the trains of wedding dresses. I tried to calm myself. I took a few deep breaths, composed my face. I turned around and walked, steadily, back to the house.

Back to Hef.

I knew then I had to leave, for real, but I had to be smarter, calmer. I had to make a plan, and I had to execute that plan. I didn't want Hef to see the fury or the defiance on my face as I walked past him in the doorway, so I lowered my head. I lowered my eyes.

I let him pat me on the back like a good girl and went to my room.

Quietly, I started setting aside some of my allowance each week. I still used some of it for the stuff I was supposed to use it on, so that Hef wouldn't notice. I made sure my clothes were up to date and my roots weren't showing. But I carved out as much as I possibly could and squirreled it away in a bank account I set up. I kept a little piece of paper in a drawer in my desk with the amount written on it. Whenever I added a bit more money, I crossed off the last figure and wrote the new one.

Slowly, the account grew.

And as it grew, so did my independence, little by little.

I was determined to start making money on my own, income from somewhere other than Hef's black pouch. It seemed like my only option was to use the one asset I had: my appearance. My body was already currency here at the mansion. My presence at the mansion itself could be lucrative for me, too, not just Hef. I began to do paid promotions on social media—campaigns for a tea that promised to make people slimmer if they drank it, teeth whitening, whatever I could find. I collaborated on a bikini line, then a loungewear line. I made an appearance as a Playmate at a show with Lil Jon, and that's all it was—an appearance. As I stood there smiling while he DJ'ed, I thought, *I have no talent.*

I'm just standing here.

There had to be something more than this. I decided after that appearance I would learn how to DJ myself, so that I was more than just an accessory.

I desperately wanted to do something real, to make something of my own. I'd always loved music, so I decided to explore it beyond DJing, maybe even try to make my own album. I didn't quite picture myself as a singer, but I wanted to try different things. I thought of my dad's beautiful voice, how his music lifted hearts and brought so much joy. I wondered if his musical talent ran in my veins, if I could sing like him after some coaching. A producer I knew set me up to do some collaborative sessions with a young musician he thought could show me the ropes.

"This is Jordan McGraw," he said, when he introduced us. "He's Dr. Phil's son, but don't judge him by that! He's a talented musician."

Jordan was indeed a talented musician. I didn't find myself attracted to him initially, but he was my age, and he paid attention to me. He asked me questions about my life and seemed genuinely interested in the answers.

The filming for the wedding special was over, but the real plans were in full motion with the staff. It was chaotic, and when I was with Jordan it felt like a safe haven. No one asked my opinion about the actual wedding ceremony. It was all being planned around me, not with me. If I wasn't in front of the cameras, it was as if I was irrelevant.

"Tell me about your dad," said Jordan. "I want to know everything about you. What you were like as a child."

I glowed under his attention. He leaned forward and gazed into my eyes while I told him about the pub and the ghosts, and I felt amazed at the words that poured out of me. I didn't feel shy or insecure. He made me feel like I was the most interesting person in the world. And the more he liked me, the more I liked him. He made me feel special, just for being me, and the contrast between that and who I was in the mansion made me giddy.

I began to trust him more and more, so I told him how anxious I was about the wedding, how fast it was progressing, how it all seemed out of my control. Three hundred people had already been invited, yet nobody had asked me to look at the guest list. RSVPs were rolling in from people like Paris Hilton and Gene Simmons. It felt like a train had left the station without me.

Jordan listened intently. "You need to talk to my dad," he said.

I drove up to Dr. Phil's house in Coldwater Canyon. The view from his couch was incredible. And he was, of course, Dr. Phil, exactly the way he looked on TV. It was like he had leaped off the screen and was sitting next to me. Surreal. He listened while I shyly, haltingly went through the basics of my situation at the mansion, then he interjected.

"Look," he said. "Here's the bottom line. You're a twenty-five-year-old woman. You're young, vibrant. You have your whole life ahead of you! You shouldn't be trapped in that house."

He's right, I thought. Here was this expert who broadcast to millions—he knew what he was talking about. I was tired of being controlled. I'd let myself get sucked into a toxic situation, and I had to get out.

Of course I had already decided that when Hef and his security prevented me from leaving, but Dr. Phil's reinforcement made me feel bolder. Stronger.

That night, I was late for curfew. It was only thirty minutes, but Hef was incensed.

"Where were you?" he screamed at me. "You're late!"

"Just driving," I said.

"Tell me where you were!"

"Just out, I lost track of time, that's all."

This made him angrier. The only other time I had seen him

like this was once, early on, when we were all out at a club and he didn't like the way I was dancing. He had grabbed my arm, hard, and yanked me down to my seat.

"Well, maybe you shouldn't be driving at all if you keep getting lost."

It didn't make sense. I hadn't said I was lost, but I was a recently empowered woman courtesy of Dr. Phil, and I was getting angry. I was a grown woman. I should be able to go where I wanted, whenever I wanted. I wasn't his staff.

So for the second time ever I turned my back and walked away from him. I didn't slam a door this time; I just quietly walked away as if what he had to say was unimportant.

This was even worse.

He came after me, enraged, and demanded I apologize.

I didn't say a word, just walked up the stairs, leaving him at the bottom staring up at me.

When he came to bed, I didn't apologize. I didn't whine and plead with him not to be angry. I turned my back to him and thought about my piece of paper with my savings listed.

It wasn't as much as I had hoped, not yet. But I was inspired at how kind Jordan and Dr. Phil were to me. Their belief in me was like cold water when you're dying of thirst.

I didn't consider that the father and son who were encouraging me to leave, to get out now, might have had an ulterior motive. Even with the blackmail, with the backstabbing in the mansion, with how many of my relationships had become transactional by nature, I was still someone who trusted first and asked questions later.

I was still me.

And if I didn't get out soon, it would be too late.

I would be married whether I wanted to be or not.

CHAPTER 13

Runaway Bride

Gradually, secretly, I moved my stuff out.

Every time I left on a short errand, I tucked some clothes and other items into a small tote bag, the kind you might take out shopping. Nothing he would notice. Nothing that would draw the attention of staff or security. Pretty soon, I was down to a couple t-shirts in a drawer. I left them there, so that if he happened to open it, it wouldn't be empty and bare and give me away.

After speaking with Dr. Phil, I'd only gotten closer and closer to Jordan. I continued to confide in him over long phone calls from my car. Or when we'd meet up to work on my music. He began flirting more and more openly, and I flirted back. When I expressed my worry over the future, over where I'd go after I escaped the mansion, I got a text from Jordan.

THIS IS FOR YOU.

Along with the text was a photo of his closet. He'd cleared out one side of it.

I stared at the photo for a long time, and then I called him.

He didn't say hello when he answered; he said, "Just move in with me."

I was silent. I liked Jordan more and more every day. I liked his dad. It seemed the easiest thing for me to do, but while we were flirty and growing closer, we weren't in the move-in-together stage. We hadn't even kissed.

But maybe, I thought, this was my transitional place. I could leave the mansion now and this would just be a place to stay as I figured out my new independent life. I still needed a job. I still needed more in my savings account.

"You need to get out," he said. "No expectations. You can leave right away, and I can spend more time with you. It's win–win." Moving in with Jordan until I could get on my feet seemed like the smart thing to do, because I was running out of time.

If little alarm bells were going off in the back of my mind, I ignored them. The looming wedding bells I needed to escape were louder.

One Saturday, in the middle of movie night, as the classic black-and-white film Hef had picked flickered over the dozens of people filling the red velvet chairs—some of them lying literally at Hef's feet, like dogs—I leaned over and whispered, "I'll be right back."

I casually slipped out like I was going to the bathroom, smiling at the guests as I walked by them. Upstairs, I tucked my last few things into my purse, then got in my car and drove out to the security booth by the front gate.

I could see the worried looks on the guards' faces because I was off script. *Crystal doesn't leave after curfew. Crystal doesn't leave in the middle of movie night.* One of the guards reached for his walkie-talkie.

"I'm just running down to Walgreens," I said quickly. "I have to pick up some tampons."

Nothing makes burly security guards more uncomfortable than

the word "tampons." The walkie-talkie went down, and the gate swung open.

I drove out.

It was June, just days before the wedding. Everything had already been ordered and paid for. The invitations, with pink crystals on them, had been handwritten in calligraphy and sent. The Romona Keveza dress had been tailored to my body. The flowers had been paid for.

A strawberry wedding cake was being baked. It was far too late to unspool all this event planning or get refunds on anything. I didn't feel guilty for sneaking away. I didn't feel guilty about the wedding. Hef had never asked me to marry him.

Going along because there's no choice and saying "yes" are two very different things.

So on a Saturday night in June I drove away from Holmby Hills. I drove away from Hef while he sat in the dark, surrounded and adored, and watched a black-and-white film where women swooned and men saved them before they delicately fluttered to the ground.

I don't know how long it took him to notice that I hadn't come back. Maybe it wasn't until he took his little pill out of its tissue and reached over to squeeze my thigh that he noticed the space next to him was empty. Or maybe another girl had sidled next to him while I was gone, and he never noticed until the lights came on.

I don't know how long he yelled at staff to find me. I imagine he raged and tantrumed and threatened to fire people if they didn't find me. I don't know if he still went to the bedroom with four or five women that night, or if his blue pill went to waste.

If he was upset it wasn't because he missed me or was worried about me. Hugh Hefner always got what he wanted when he wanted it.

When I was five miles away from the mansion I pulled over, and in the last light of the day I pulled out from my purse a red lipstick I had bought at the drugstore the day before and slowly put it on in the rearview mirror. Hef may have hated red lipstick on a woman.

But he hated defiance even more.

In the days that followed, the tabloids reported that Hef had lost a quarter of a million dollars on the canceled wedding.

I ran straight to Jordan and hid from it all.

I turned off my phone.

When Jordan kissed me for the first time, I felt butterflies. It reminded me of Greg a little bit.

As soon as I had unpacked my stuff Jordan began talking about forever. It was overwhelming but in a good way. He wrote me little love notes and put them everywhere; he showered me with affection and compliments constantly. It was such a contrast to my time with Hef that I became drunk on his love for me.

It got intense, fast. We spent all our time together; I didn't really have anyone else. There was always an element of overdoing it. It was too perfect, too much, too sweet, like cotton candy. It was the nuclear version of love-bombing. The first time he went away for the weekend without me, he filled the entire house with ten thousand dollars' worth of roses. He had his dad's black Amex and he used it . . . a lot.

But I wanted so badly for it to work out. I thought, *This is it. This is love.* So much was resting on the shoulders of this relationship. It symbolized my freedom, my escape. I didn't just want it to work out—I *needed* it to work out.

Maybe, I thought, all my time at the mansion was just so I could meet Jordan. Maybe he was my fairy tale, my real-life prince like in *Enchanted.* Jordan and his dad made me feel empowered enough to leave Hef, but I quickly gave my power back again. I had sworn

I would stay sober from depending on a man, but I relapsed at the first empty closet I saw.

Like so many girls raised in this culture, I was still looking for someone to save me, to make me feel valuable and worthy. I had left the mansion, but I hadn't spent a minute alone. I hadn't done any work on myself, and I made the same mistake again. I ran from one man to another, hoping it would fix all my problems.

In July, a month after I'd driven to Walgreens "for tampons," the issue of *Playboy* with my cover came out. Like the wedding, it had been much too late to pull the cover, or even change the headline. So there it was, exactly as they'd sent it to the printers: me in Hef's captain's hat, in his silk robe, on his leather armchair. "America's Princess" read the big block letters, "Introducing Mrs. Crystal Hefner!"

Except Hef had had them print hundreds of thousands of red stickers and slap them on the cover, right on top of my body.

The stickers said: *RUNAWAY BRIDE IN THIS ISSUE!*

It seemed like those magazines were everywhere, bright red stickers blaring. It was Hef's own branded version of a scarlet letter.

I tried to sell my engagement ring. I didn't want it anymore—it felt like a curse. And I needed the money. It quickly became apparent that the money I'd saved wasn't going to last very long. I reached out to a friend from San Diego who had a jewelry shop—I needed to go somewhere that would be discreet, where I could trust them not to photograph me or call the media. When I showed up at the arranged time, they were acting strange. Stiff. Before my internal alarm bells could go off, paparazzi leaped out from behind the counter and started wildly snapping photos. I whirled around and ran out, but it was too late—the pictures of me trying to pawn my ring were all over TMZ within the hour. I looked like an opportunist, a money-hungry jilting bride. Some outlets ran stories that I'd been cheating on Hef with Jordan before I'd left. Every sordid thing they could think to say about me, they said. I wanted to scream, *This isn't me! This isn't how it was!* But nobody cared. They wanted black-and-white, not gray. High-gloss drama, not nuance. Salacious sound bites, not complicated real life. Everybody was in business, everybody was trying to make a living, and this was the stuff that sold copy. I knew that. But it still hurt.

I gave a few interviews, but I glossed over everything. I tried to put the best spin possible on things, for Hef. Even then, I was still doing his bidding—making sure he came out looking good. *Be loving toward me. Make me look good. Wear the flag.*

I was still programmed to sell the *Playboy* brand.

"It was a mutual decision," I told Ryan Seacrest.

The one time I broke from that and let Howard Stern coax me into saying cruel things about Hef, I felt awful about it after. I'd tried to make myself feel better by dogging on mansion life, but I only felt worse, like I'd lowered myself even further into a pit of shame and regret.

I found myself, strangely, worrying about Hef, wondering if he was okay. I should have been worrying about the damage he was doing to the girlfriends who were there now, but instead, like some kind of kidnap victim with Stockholm syndrome, I was worrying about him. Right before I'd left, I'd pulled Paige aside and asked her to take care of him if anything ever happened to me. "You have to really watch out for him," I'd said. "Promise me."

I didn't love Hef, and in many ways I was angry with him, but I still cared about him for all the complicated reasons you care about someone when you shouldn't. Just because I couldn't marry him didn't mean I wanted anything bad to happen to him. I still had a heart, or maybe I had just been trained and conditioned to care about his happiness. But either way, I found myself worrying about him at odd times. I wondered if there were new girls taking advantage of him. I thought of him missing me, and I was surprised to find my eyes fill up with tears at the idea of him doing something so out of character.

Paige had promised to watch out for Hef, but it was in a throwaway manner.

"Nothing's going to happen to you," she said.

"But if anything does, you just need to make sure he's okay."

"Okay, fine. But I really want a BMW, so if I promise you, will you promise to plant the seed with him?"

I didn't really trust Paige anymore, but she was the only girlfriend in the house I could ask to look out for him. When she'd first moved in, we had so much fun together—staying up late, talking about our childhoods, connecting. One night we ran around the mansion like kids at a sleepover, giggling and whispering; she'd pulled her skirt up and hoisted her bare butt up, pressed it against the painting in the dining room, the Jackson Pollock. I laughed so hard I cried. I remember thinking, *Finally, a real friend here!* But soon she started asking me for stuff, pressuring me to ask Hef to give her money, or a *Playboy* pictorial, and now a BMW.

It was sad to me that yet another person I had hoped would be a friend, an ally, was just trying to get something out of me like everyone else. I desperately wanted to have more female friends, but they broke my heart and my trust as much as men did.

In the tabloids and on Twitter, Hef effortlessly played the victim. He came across as slightly wounded, but still "the man" with a thousand girlfriends. He said he was blindsided, that he didn't see it coming. "She didn't even tell Paige, and that's her best friend," he told one tabloid.

Of course I hadn't told her I was leaving. She would have used the information to get her BMW. There was no one I could have trusted in the mansion with my secret.

As the weeks went on, the hubbub in the media surrounding our breakup died down. Everybody moved on. So I tried to forge ahead. I'd gotten out of the mansion—now here was my chance to have a real life, a happy life.

Things started to sour pretty quickly with Jordan. His displays of affection were still over the top, but there was an emptiness at the core of it. I had a nagging sense that something wasn't genuine, that I couldn't really trust him, but I chalked it up to my own insecurity and fear. I knew trust was hard for me, but I still felt this growing unease that his love was fickle, that all the over-the-top displays weren't really about me.

For his birthday, I threw Jordan a surprise party. He found out about it ahead of time, and I realized he'd caught on. *Oh, well,* I thought. But when the party night rolled around, he made a big elaborate show of pretending he was surprised, and would not drop the performance, even for me. There was something disturbing about it—when he wouldn't admit to this small thing and give up the charade, it felt deeply deceptive. I wondered what else he was capable of. I felt a cold wave of recognition: another performer. Another fake relationship. I had no idea, really, who this person actually was. Once again I was living with a man I barely knew. There were shades of Owen in him, even though they lived in different worlds and had nothing in common outwardly.

Jordan desperately wanted to be in a band, and one day we were at the Viper Room in Hollywood where he was auditioning lead singers, and Dr. Phil came in to watch. Jordan and I were sitting next to each other in front of the stage, and Dr. Phil stood behind us talking with a few of the stage managers and staff of the Viper Room.

"Look at my son," I heard him say, "He bagged himself a Playmate."

The men all laughed. I thought about the day Dr. Phil had told me I had more value than just being Hugh Hefner's wife. I remembered how it felt when he and Jordan said they believed in me.

I felt stupid for thinking anyone valued me for anything real. I was just a thing to be bagged to him. He had fooled me, too.

I latched onto Jordan and his family like I was drowning, and they were my life preserver. I couldn't keep up with how they spent money, though—their lifestyle almost made the mansion look like a monastery. I was wary of Dr. Phil after hearing him objectify me, but I was even more wary of Jordan's mom. In my mind, she and Jordan had an overly enmeshed and codependent relationship.

When I wanted to do something special for Jordan's birthday, I surprised him with tickets to see *Book of Mormon* in New York City. When I handed him his gift he opened it and he cried, but I found out later that his mom had already told him about my gift, because she knew he didn't like surprises.

Jordan told his mom he needed a bigger house to listen to his records in, so he moved into a $6 million mansion in Beverly Hills. He loved Disney movies like I did, so he, or his parents, built an exact replica of the fountain from *Nightmare Before Christmas* and had it installed in front of the house. I was in awe. We decorated the house with his unlimited daddy money, and it was nothing but excess: Be@rbrick figurines, toys really, that cost five thousand dollars each, a diamond-dusted painting of Kurt Cobain, every kind of toy you could imagine. Everything was over the top, and he always had to have the latest and greatest thing, whether it was electronics or music equipment or memorabilia. As long as it was bigger and better than anyone else had, he wanted it. And his parents bought it for him. We even had a 50,000-piece jigsaw puzzle spread out on our massive dining room table.

I was free of the mansion while living with Jordan, but I didn't feel free. I wasn't independent. I wasn't in charge of my life. I wasn't really making my own decisions. All of my attachment issues, abandonment issues, and self-esteem issues were on full display in our house next to the custom duck figurines he made and displayed all over the house because his pet name for me was "duck."

As the months went on with Jordan, the love bombing and Prince Charming behavior lessened. He started trashing hotel rooms like a pretend rockstar—it seemed to me he desperately wanted to be Tommy Lee, and he wanted me to be his Pamela Anderson. He was spoiled and immature. When I complained about how he acted, especially out in public, he started going on more trips without me. When he was gone I wandered around his glassy and glossy house feeling untethered and afraid. I started getting paranoid he was going to leave me. I berated myself for berating him.

One night while he was away, my trust issues got the best of me, and I looked at his old phone. He had just gotten a new one, and when I saw the old one I couldn't help myself. I had never been someone to go through anyone's private things, but I wanted to know if my growing unease was based in reality or just something I was going to have to work on in therapy someday soon. The phone was still connected to the Internet so I could see all his most recent emails on the screen. One of them from his mom had the subject line: CRYSTAL.

In the email she was advising him that it was better to break up with me sooner rather than later, saying it was better to do it after one year rather than two. I read email after email of her doubting I was good enough for him. She was encouraging her son to end things. She babied and coddled him in a way that would have made a great episode of the *Dr. Phil* show.

I was used to competing with other women, but I had never competed with someone's mother. It was awkward at best, and pathological at worst.

In one email she even offered to break up with me for him.

I felt sick to my stomach. I had hoped to find a real man, but instead I had hooked up with a little boy who needed his mommy to do his dirty work for him.

I felt more lost than ever. I had wasted the freedom I had fought so hard for on yet another broken man. I had spent all of my money trying to match the lifestyle of this rich and kinda famous family, and on trying to buy Jordan more extravagant presents than his mom did.

I packed up only the things in the house that were mine and left everything else and anything that was mine but was a memento or reminder of our relationship. I was devastated that I had failed yet again. But I was determined to leave before I was left, so in a way it felt like progress.

When Jordan saw that I had moved out he texted me: *YOU LEFT ALL THE DUCK STUFF.* I think that may have hurt him the most. I want to say I was cavalier about the breakup, I want to say that after losing Greg and leaving Hef, leaving Jordan was no big deal. But it was a very big deal.

At the time it felt like the most devastating and hardest breakup of my life. I had been desperately, delusionally, committed to the idea that Jordan was the one, because if he was the one then that gave meaning to everything I had gone through at the mansion.

I could call it fate or destiny, I could say I never would have met Jordan if I hadn't been in *Playboy*, if I hadn't been Hef's number one girlfriend. Disney movies and *Casablanca* nights had programmed me into believing that there was always a happily-ever-after involving a man.

There was no Disney movie where the princess, feeling sad and rejected and alone, runs away from not one but two mansions, and moves into a condo in Sherman Oaks with nothing but her poor life choices and a mounting stack of bills to keep her company.

I had no job and a very real need for a way to support myself. What little I had left in savings I had decided to invest in a lingerie business with a girl I had met at the mansion. We rented a location, ordered stock, opened a brick-and-mortar store, became friends... but within months, the whole thing crumbled. We didn't work as business partners, and the venture failed, and our friendship failed.

I had spent six months outside the mansion failing spectacularly at everything I tried.

I had nothing to show for it. Nothing. Everything had fallen apart. My relationship. My friendship. My business.

Everything I'd feared would happen had come to pass: I'd destroyed my future by living at the mansion as a girlfriend. I was now one of Hef's many conquests, and nothing more. Worse: I was the one who walked away from a *Playboy* cover and a marriage proposal. I looked back at my life and saw nothing but a string of bad choices and missteps. Dating the wrong people. Seeking approval in the wrong places. Agreeing to things I never should have agreed to. Giving up on life at the mansion before I'd gotten anywhere. At least when I was there, I'd been part of that bubble of protection and fame. People didn't mess with me because they didn't want to mess with Hef. The public cared about the things I did: what I wore, whether I DJ'ed a party, if I fought with another girlfriend. Sure, it was toxic, but people were interested at least. It made me feel that I mattered, in some way. Now, I was just invisible.

Except to a certain foreign prince, who was calling my mom nonstop and offering her $400,000 if I traveled to see him in his country. The money thrilled my mom, but it felt sinister and dangerous to me. It felt like he was offering to buy me, and maybe he was.

My life outside the mansion without Jordan, without anyone, felt chaotic and sad and now with this foreign prince lurking, it also felt dangerous in a new way. I felt unprotected and vulnerable, so in my head I began to rewrite history. Life at the mansion hadn't been so bad. They had never really aggressively prevented me from leaving. I had it pretty good there. Curfews are safer because nothing really good happens after nine-thirty p.m.—that's true. Why did I want to escape? What was I thinking?

I was consumed with regret and doubt, and then, once again, my phone rang.

This time it wasn't Hef on the other end of the line. It was Mary. Her brash, smoky voice on the phone immediately made me homesick for the mansion. I couldn't believe I was thinking that, after feeling so trapped there for so long, after fighting my way out. But that's how I felt. Things were not going well for me on the outside. So when Mary launched in about how much Hef missed me, I felt myself softening more quickly than I would have liked.

She told me he was lonely and lost without me, and while I didn't know if that was true, I suddenly wished for it to be true. I was so susceptible to being wanted, like I always had been. When someone wanted me, I suddenly felt valuable. It was an incredible feeling, like the rush of a drug—but it could drain away just as fast. It wasn't healthy. But I was hungry for it.

And, it turned out, he'd been calling my mom. My mom had always loved Hef. She told anyone she could that "Hugh Hefner is my son-in-law." It tickled her to no end. And she loved being able to come and go at the mansion.

"He was *in tears* to me on the phone the other day," my mom said to me. "Give him another chance, Crystal. What on earth are you doing out here?"

Mary called me too and said basically the same thing, that Hef wasn't happy without me. He was distraught. There were tears. I doubted Hef was actually in tears, and a part of me knew Mary was trying to manipulate me, but it was nice to imagine him crying over me.

Honestly, I didn't know what on earth I *was* doing. I was stressed all the time. I felt like a walking nerve, coursing with anxiety. I had lost weight; I was so skinny. And bitterly, I felt that I'd been convinced by bad actors to give up something I shouldn't have let go of. Dr. Phil's words on his couch on the day that Jordan sent me up there to him started to seem so sinister—not a kind man giving good advice, but an entitled man used to getting his way, trying to get his son something he wanted.

So I did it. I went back.

I told Hef, "I've grown up a lot."

Hef told me, "You don't know what you've got until it's gone. I didn't know how much I'd miss you."

A part of me knew that what he missed about me was not *me*, but the idea of me, of having me around. He didn't like that I left him, so he needed me to come back, to right that wrong. Crystal

Harris didn't leave Hugh Hefner, and even if he just needed me to make that true, it still felt good to be needed. It was effortless to step back into my life in the mansion and forget my time away.

Okay, I thought. *I can do this again. But better this time.*

Because now Hef was afraid of me leaving, and that little power was power enough.

I cleaned out the other girlfriends. There would be no more of this constant competition with other women, Hef making his manipulative little comments to pit us against one another, or make us feel lesser than another woman in his eyes. I knew how to play the game now—how to navigate the politics of the mansion. And I knew how to get rid of girls I didn't like. Hef hated drama among the girlfriends—as much as he liked us to feel competitive with one another for his attention, he found it distasteful when things erupted. All it really took was subtly calling his attention to some volcanic conflicts that were emerging among the girls, and they were out.

He still wanted sex to be a group activity, though—and that, while distasteful, was better than the alternative. The handful of times he tried to be romantic or intimate with me, only me . . . it was just awkward. It was clear he had no idea how to do it. And truth be told, the last thing I wanted was to have sex with him alone.

There was one person I knew I could really trust at the mansion. I called Amber.

She drove up to the mansion to help me out. She stayed for the weekend. We swam in the pool, caught up on life. Things had been up and down for her, as they had for me. Life was turning out to be harder and more complicated than either of us would have guessed that night we first met.

And each night, when it was time to go up to the bedroom, she came, too. I was grateful.

Before she left, I prodded Hef.

"Do you have some gas money for Amber? She drove a long way to visit."

We were still pretending that what was happening was not happening.

"Oh, right," he said, and unlocked the cabinet with the wooden box. He counted out a few thousand dollars. Gas money.

The mansion was still a twisted underworld. But at least now, I felt a little bit in control.

Then one day, as I stood in the office chatting with Mary, she said something that stopped me in my tracks. She was flipping through some old files full of photos—Hef always kept photos of the girls who came to the mansion, marking each with a letter A through D, to rate their attractiveness—and talking about the girlfriends who'd flowed in and out of the mansion over the years. She'd been there for a long time, closing in on forty years, so she'd seen all the turnover, all the churn, all the young girls showing up, getting their nose jobs and boob jobs and begging for a shot in the magazine, and then getting spat out the other side.

She looked down at one picture, shook her head, and said, "He always keeps the ones with the broken wings."

Was that me? I'd left, but I hadn't been able to fly. In the time since I'd come back to the mansion, I'd been thinking that I finally had my hand on the tiller of my own life, that I was steering instead of just getting swept along. I thought I was on top of things. But maybe I was just another bird with broken wings.

Or maybe I wasn't a bird at all.

Maybe I was just broken.

And this house was exactly where I belonged.

CHAPTER 14

Now Playing the Role of Wife

We got married on New Year's Eve 2012. The last day of the year.

I was twenty-six years old; he was eighty-six.

He wore a black tuxedo with a pink tulip in his lapel. I wore a strapless pale pink dress with a skirt made of soft ruffles that looked almost like crushed roses, all the way to the floor. The publicist from *Playboy* had brought over a stack of bridal magazines, and I picked the first one I saw when I opened the cover. I liked that it was pink. I told myself that when I got married for real someday, I would wear a white dress.

The morning of the wedding, I'd pulled out my phone and tapped out a tweet.

> *Today is the day I become Mrs. Hugh Hefner.*
> *Feeling very happy, lucky, and blessed.*

To exchange vows, we stood under an archway of white and pink flowers mounted to the double curving staircase in the heart of the Playboy Mansion. The stairs I had walked up in my French maid costume a lifetime ago, in the thrall of the man in the silk smoking jacket, leading the parade of willing girls. We held hands. He seemed way older to me than he had a little over a year ago when he proposed the first time, like time was catching up to him. He was a little pale, a little stooped.

There were only ten people at the wedding besides us. There were my mom and my stepdad, Ted, whom she'd been married to for a while now, and whom I had really come to love. I'd gotten to know him; he was a kind man. And Hef's brother and his wife, plus a few other of his friends and family. After the ceremony, we had a champagne toast and cut the cake. I felt proud that it was small and reserved, like a sweet old-fashioned wedding from long ago—the opposite of the splashy, celebrity-studded publicity fest that the *Playboy* machine had originally planned. At that point I was beyond dwelling on the fact that my groom was sixty years older than me, and that my feelings toward him could only be described as complicated. I had gotten very good at not thinking too hard about things.

Back in December, a few weeks before the wedding, I'd gotten the prenup paperwork from Hef and the Playboy Foundation. There was nothing there that was surprising to me: It awarded me very little relative to his net worth. The foundation controlled most of Hef's money, not him. And they really didn't want me to have any of it. There were pages and pages of fine print detailing what I was not entitled to. They even made sure to note that I had no right to use the bunny head logo.

I brought the prenup to a lawyer to have it notarized.

"I can't let you sign this," he said. "It's grossly unfair to you."

I didn't care. I wasn't trying to make it fair, I was just trying to get it done. So I brought it to a different lawyer, who didn't argue when I told him I didn't want to negotiate.

He helped me sign and notarize it, and that was that.

After we got married, things were different. Hef seemed to respect me more. And because I wasn't afraid of being kicked out, I began to take back even more of my own power and agency. I was no longer on the chopping block, so he couldn't use that to control me. That nervousness of impermanence was gone—I was a part of this place now, for better or worse.

He knew it.

I knew it.

And so we settled in.

When people came to the mansion, he actually introduced me. It used to be that I was the unmentioned prop, something you'd no more talk about or call attention to than the watch on your wrist. Now he said, "Have you met my wife?"

It felt like progress. It was a small thing, but it felt like a win.

Back when it was a crowd of *Playboy* girlfriends in the mansion, all of us going out together, we used to talk among ourselves, even if it stayed a bit superficial and was always calculated. As much as we were set up to be competitive and back-stabby with one another, there was a part of us that wanted connection. We all wanted friends, especially friends who were going through the same thing. It was such a double-edged sword: We knew these girls would push us off a cliff to have our spot at the mansion, but at the same time, we wanted a friend, and this was our only group to choose from.

My only real friend among the other girls was Amber. She was not invited to the wedding because Hef insisted it be only family and a few of his friends, so Mary stood as my maid of honor.

When I was first living there, I listened closely to the things the other girls talked about and tried hard to figure out what was normal and what was totally off the wall. It was hard to tell. They would talk about plastic surgery the way they talked about getting their nails done, so casually. A lot of them got labiaplasties. They just had their lips sliced right off. "I don't want anything hanging!"

And when it came to success, they could be coldly realistic, even if it sounded retro. "A lot of it is who you marry," they would say.

What I knew: When you have no money, nobody cares about you. I'd seen my parents go through that. I'd gone through that. When you're poor and you live paycheck to paycheck, or exist off someone else's grudging generosity—when they make sure you know exactly what they're giving you and want you to be grateful—I knew how that felt. And I knew that when you have money, you have power. You have people's attention. So when you come from nothing and you get access to money, you go from feeling like a speck of nothing to feeling very valuable.

And now that I was *Mrs. Hefner,* at least I had something: I had that name. I had a stamp of legitimacy that I'd never had as a girlfriend.

As Hef's wife, I suddenly didn't have to say yes to everything or accommodate his every whim. I had more agency, more free will, but I had to pick my battles. The systems at the mansion were still entirely built around Hef, even though we were married. Everything was still set up to facilitate his desires. The staff still eased the way. At parties, they put certain girls in certain rooms, closer to him; they served drinks at opportune times. If he was interested in someone, they made sure the wheels were greased for her to stay, for her to end up in the bedroom with us. The office staff combed through hundreds of photos ahead of the weekends, marking the ones they knew he would like for an invitation—one of them had chosen me, five years before. They made sure his gas envelope was filled with cash. And most of all, everyone participated in this as though it were entirely normal. As though there were nothing abhorrent about the commerce of women, about choosing them like appetizers off a menu. Just another day at the mansion for Hef. Marriage didn't change anything in that regard, and I was fine with it.

Being Hef's wife was, in some ways, a job just like being a girlfriend had been. The job was still to keep the *Playboy* mythology afloat, to protect Hef's image, and to be everything he needed, every minute, always. It was a job, but it felt like a promotion.

Things were the same as before I left, but the act of leaving changed something in Hef's impression of me. I had pierced his self-image. He was a man no woman would ever leave, and because I did, he respected me; and Hef never had respect for women. Not really. Not in any way that would actually feel like respect to a woman.

I also think he was just a little bit afraid of me, and the possibility I could rock his carefully controlled world again.

I had to control access to Hef more and more. Everybody wanted something from him. If someone came up to me at a mansion event and wanted to chat, there was a 99.9 percent chance they wanted to get to him through me. Nobody, ever, wanted to talk to me just to talk to me. I was nothing to them but a doorway to Hef. One night, for movie night, some regulars brought a new person, this lovely older woman who was small and wiry and seemed friendly and warm. They all came up to me to talk at the end of the night to introduce her—she was ninety years old, still did yoga every day, had written a book about it.

"Here's my book," she said to me, pressing it into my hands. "I want you to have it."

I was touched—it was so unusual for people to think of me or what I'd be interested in. But when they left, I flipped it open, and saw that it was addressed to Hef, with a long note hoping he would promote the book. I shut the book and set it aside and scolded myself for falling for it. That kind of stuff happened all the time, every night of the week. I was tired of it. So I put up walls. I smiled and performed the role of wife and hostess, but I put a protective distance between me and anybody else. Everybody had a motive.

I also, in a strange role reversal, began to protect Hef.

Now that I was the wife, I began organizing the mansion. There were decades' worth of disarray and clutter. I didn't have a job outside, and now that the mansion was my permanent home, I began a form of nesting. I sorted the vast numbers of photos and scrapbooks and videos and memorabilia. I was now part of Hef's legacy, and his legacy was in disarray. Hef would get so many gifts—really expensive gifts from amazing artists, from corporations, from celebrities, from educational institutions. A doctor even gave him a lock of Michael Jackson's hair. When Hef received a gift, he instructed the staff to "put the gift in storage." When I went to catalogue the millions of dollars of gifts that were supposed to have been put in storage at the mansion, there was nothing there. The storage room was empty except for a few trinkets of little to no value—a child's music box, some cheap snow globes, some random movie memorabilia. I didn't have the heart to tell him everything was gone, that people he had trusted had betrayed his trust. I told Jennifer, the new secretary who had been hired to help Mary. Mary was almost as old as Hef, but like Hef, she never planned to retire.

Jennifer had become a close friend. She was smart and close to my age, and was the first woman in the mansion who I felt was actually on my side. She had boundaries between her work life and her personal life and held them strongly. Unlike Mary, she didn't get caught up in the drama. Her job was just her job, and I admired her for that.

I asked Jennifer not to tell Hef everything was gone. It would have broken his heart.

His staff, who were supposed to be like family, or his friends, or his special guests, or his actual family—there was no way to know—had stolen it all. I knew he would never go there in his lifetime, so I kept the secret. But I put a lock on the door, and when new gifts came I catalogued them, I computerized the entries, I subtly let the staff know his estate attorney had a copy of everything in storage and I was the only one who had the key.

Hef was too trusting of the people on his payroll. He would sign stacks of papers without looking at them. I tried to warn him about this.

"Do you read through these documents all the way?" I asked. "I think you need to know exactly what you're signing."

"We need to trust the people who work for us," he said dismissively.

I thought about the empty vault, but blind trust in people was the one thing my husband and I had in common.

The difference was that I was also paranoid, certain that everyone was trying to take advantage of me while at the same time assuming the best of everyone.

Hef couldn't imagine anyone having the audacity to cross him, or steal from him, or disrespect him. His ignorance was his bliss.

When he started getting less coherent and falling asleep in the middle of game nights and movie nights, we decided to check on the earthquake supplies. I unlocked his special cabinet in the bedroom to check on them, and they were gone, all of them, bottles and bottles of pain pills just empty. The reality of his addiction, his massive tolerance level, and how much they were affecting him made everyone finally decide to control his access. No more earthquake supply. With so many celebrities dying of overdoses from doctors who gave them endless supplies, people around him got more careful, and the opiates had to be given to him like he used to give us allowance—in controlled doses.

I put an end to the demoralizing allowance ritual once we were married—instead arranging for direct deposit of my allowance, so I didn't have to hold my hand out and beg. I submitted my credit card bills to the office, and the office paid them for me. It was a bit more freedom, and a little bit more self-respect, but I was still saving every penny I could. The prenup meant that should Hef and I get divorced, I would walk away with virtually nothing. So I saved and I learned how to invest in the stock market. I formed an LLC, studied real estate, and bought first one house and then another—fixer-uppers that I could flip or rent out. I learned about passive income and did my best to create various income streams. I DJ'ed every Saturday in Vegas at the Hard Rock for $7,500. Hef flew me there in the morning and was fine with this side hustle as long as I was back for movie night.

I grew my social media. I studied emerging crypto currencies and began building a separate financial portfolio. I got some brand sponsorships. As I worked hard to become a savvy businesswoman,

I kept all of this, the rental properties, the day trading, the business partnerships a secret from everyone. I vowed to never rely on anyone else again for my financial security.

It wasn't easy, but I studied and I learned. I started creating social media channels for him—teaching him how to tweet and then eventually tweeting for him. He wasn't even close to being a digital native, but I knew that every tweet he sent would be a part of his legacy, a part of history. I also advised him on the Playmates he selected for the magazine, going over the narrowed-down choices the new editors sent over.

He began to rely on me more and more.

My role as wife at first was to be there for Hef: Be the sparkly blonde who was always right there at his elbow, a beautiful, silent accessory. But soon I was there at his elbow holding his arm to support him so when we were out in public, nobody would know he was starting to get frail or confused. I supported him as discreetly as I could to make sure nobody would notice. He trusted me, and that felt good. I wasn't going to let him down. He began to depend on me physically and also depend on me to hide the big secret he was still trying to keep: He was aging and diminishing, and no number of young girls surrounding him could reverse that or make it not true. Everybody knew, of course, but my job was to help him believe that nobody could tell.

I also began to feel a growing sense of responsibility to his place in cultural history. He was Hugh Hefner, an icon, a legend; and I didn't want the man he was becoming to erase the man he had been. It was a fine line to walk.

I had to be the perfect wife, and I still had to have the perfect body. I was good at being the perfect wife. I was incredibly busy being the perfect wife.

We grew closer and closer keeping up the pretense that the schedule he had created for his life was still manageable. Most of it was, but he tired more easily. He was slightly less rigid.

He loved that I was going through all the scrapbooks, and when I was organizing them he would sit and look through them one at a time, telling me stories from decade after decade.

I liked this side of him. He was like an elder giving an oral history, albeit a really sexy oral history. He was still a narcissist and still only thought of his own needs and comfort, but when he told stories inspired by the pages of his scrapbooks, there was a little glimmer now and then of something real, something maybe even a tiny bit vulnerable.

We worked for hours, side by side, and grew a little more familiar and comfortable. We became just a little more real to each other. It was strange. After so much time together, after getting married, we were finally getting to know each other.

But then, I got sick.

CHAPTER 15

In Sickness and in Health

It started with a feeling of heaviness. It was as if gravity were pulling on me a little harder than usual. I felt sluggish, like my bones were made of lead.

I'm just tired, I thought.

But I was napping all the time. I'd lie down for a minute in the bedroom and wake up hours later. I had to keep canceling things. I felt lazy and ashamed that I couldn't just get up and get back with it. But just walking felt like swimming through thick water. My stomach was upset all the time, and especially if I tried to eat anything. I felt like I was allergic to all food, any food; like there was a war in my body. This went on for months; it got worse. And when I went to the doctor, they dismissed me at first. *It's stress,* they said. *You're depressed,* they said.

My symptoms were extensive and varied: brain fog, poor memory, clicking in my wrists, joint pain, bladder pain, bone pain, so many kinds of pain. I felt like my veins were on fire, like my blood was heating up my skin. I had heart palpitations, night sweats, and I couldn't regulate my own body temperature. I was cold, then hot, then cold. I lost weight; my hair was falling out. My neck was stiff. I was moody. One minute I was jumpy and anxious, and the next I was depressed and lethargic. I had issues with my balance, and of course there was the never-ending, relentless fatigue.

But the doctor still said it was stress.

Stress is what they call a "wastebasket diagnosis." A wastebasket diagnosis is where a person can actually be sick but the doctor doesn't know what's wrong with them, so they land on a bogus conclusion just to have a diagnosis.

Stress was having to look a certain way all the time. Stress was getting abused in the media. Stress was trying to make curfew when all you want to do is watch a summer sunset by the beach. Stress is having to fake sexual pleasure when you are feeling disgusted. I knew stress, and this was not stress.

I started thinking I might be dying.

Oh well, I thought. *I've lived a lot of life.* I was too exhausted to really care.

I took my diagnosis and went to a holistic gastrointestinal doctor who performed countless tests, gave me a long list of supplements to take for the deficiencies the testing revealed in my body, and also put me on a better diet.

He then asked me if I'd ever been around ticks.

"Ticks?" I said, confused.

"This sounds like Lyme disease," he said. "Let's run some tests."

Lyme disease testing was expensive, around $1,500, but he recommended that I do the test just so we could at least rule it out. I declined, knowing that I couldn't possibly have Lyme disease—I had always been a beach girl, and there aren't ticks at the beach.

After my visit, my health actually got worse due to something he called "Herxing." Herxing is when you start cleaning up your diet and taking supplements or antibiotics, and your body starts detoxifying, and it makes you feel worse. I don't know if that was what was going on medically, but it did feel like every cell in my body had turned on me.

By late 2015 I was bedridden, and my iron levels were so low I had to start IV transfusions. I ended up taking the Lyme disease test, and I tested positive for Borrelia—the main Lyme bacteria—Bartonella, and Babesia. Bartonella is what they call the cat-scratch disease, and Babesia is a cousin to malaria. I was a mess. The bacteria involved in Lyme disease is the same shape as syphilis, strangely enough, and because it's a spirally, twisted bacteria, it multiplies and corkscrews its way into everything inside your body—muscle, bone, brain, soft tissue—anywhere and everywhere it can infiltrate, it does. So much damage from a little tick that I hadn't even noticed had been on me.

After my Lyme diagnosis, the doctors began taking me seriously. They dug deeper and found that almost everything in my body was out of whack. My thyroid and adrenals had tanked. Hormone levels were way off. Not only had these tick-borne bacteria proliferated in my body, but my body was also attacking itself. It was the implants.

Doctors were starting to see this more and more: Women who'd had implants put in years before were showing up with these mysterious and hard-to-pin-down clusters of symptoms. But they all pointed to an autoimmune disruption: the body turning against itself. I remembered the surgery I'd had in my first year at the mansion, when the surgeon had talked about my body attacking the implant, building scar tissue around it. I remembered how that scar tissue looked when they sliced me open, pulled out the inflatable silicone bag, and scraped my tissue off it. Like hamburger. And then they'd put it right back in.

I not only had Lyme disease, but also breast implant illness, and my blood work and symptoms also suggested toxic mold exposure. That could only be coming from one place: the mansion.

I hired someone to come into the mansion and take a look. He got up on a ladder, pulled one vent off, and frowned.

"This place is absolutely full of black mold," he said.

It was everywhere.

This whole time, the mansion had been breaking me down, one way or another. Now it was breaking down my health, my body. The house itself was literally making me sick. The funniest thing to me—darkly funny—was the way Hef had always insisted that the mansion was better than the outside world, right down to the air. He would actually say, "The air is better in here." And the whole time, it was the air that was poison.

I remembered when I first moved into the mansion, and it rained. All over the house the water seeped in from the roof, the walls, the windows. It had seemed like the entire mansion was weeping. It was never fixed, and every time it rained the dripping could be heard everywhere.

They fumigated the whole house for black mold, but it was so hard to eradicate. Like the spiral bacterium hiding in my blood, in my joints, it had infected every nook and cranny of the mansion. The growth turned out to be worst in the vent right above my desk in the vanity, where I liked to sit alone, thinking I was safe in my one refuge in that house.

I started a six-month course of IV antibiotics to try to knock the Lyme disease and co-infections out. And when I had any energy,

I continued cleaning out the mansion. Hef had become such a hoarder, there was junk everywhere. Piles of paperwork, files, and articles he'd clipped, so much that you could barely move around it in his bedroom and in the office, which was up a spiral staircase from the bedroom. I started there and worked my way down. I combed through everything. I organized. I boxed stuff up and put it into storage. I documented and catalogued everything.

The good photos of Hef and his girlfriends, articles about him, anything *Playboy*-related, I set aside for the scrapbooks. Hef saved and carefully preserved everything that had anything to do with him. There were two mansion employees, Peggy and Stu, whose entire jobs involved scouring the newspapers and Internet for content about Hef and memorializing it. Every Saturday, for the entire decade I'd lived at the mansion, the office printed out anything and everything that had popped up that week about Hef or *Playboy*. Stu or Peggy would read through it, screen out the negative stuff—although Hef liked the negative stuff just as much, and put it into the scrapbooks along with the puff pieces and the nude pictures of his girlfriends and Playmates—and type up captions for every photo or article.

There were, at that point, more than three thousand scrapbooks documenting Hef's life. He always said he was doing it for posterity. For history. In his mind, he was so legendary and iconic, future historians were going to need this incessant documentation of his life. He had no idea what was coming, in terms of the sea change in public opinion toward men like him.

And then I found the photos. Entire shoeboxes full of photos from disposable cameras, the kind you had to take to a drugstore to develop. I remembered Hef clutching a cheap plastic Kodak on those nights out, calling for us to lift our shirts. And there it all was. The dark inside of a limo, girls with their skirts pulled up and their legs spread open, an overly bright flash on pale exposed skin. I recognized all these girls, some of whom I'd overlapped with. Some I'd been friendly with, some had been my enemies, had hated me and trash-talked me to the press. Some had gone on to find success and fame; some had simply vanished. Here were Holly, Bridget, Kendra, the twins. Paige, whose face it still stung a little to see. So many others. The limo photos went back years. Decades.

I shredded them. All of them. I tore them apart by hand, into thousands of tiny pieces that fell to the floor around me like snow, until my fingers ached.

It took hours.

Hef was slowing down. The sex stopped altogether in 2014, even before I got sick, and I was relieved. There was no more going out, no more bringing girls home, no more performances. For years, I had been keeping up the *Playboy* Playmate charade, for Hef, for the public. I couldn't do it anymore. I was too tired. I was too sick. So I stopped.

I stopped faking that I was fine. I was not fine.

I stopped dyeing my hair. My brown roots grew in.

I took everything fake out of my body. I scheduled a surgery and had the implants taken out. It took eight years for me to realize I was getting sick from my implants. My body had been trying to tell me they had to go since I first went to the mansion, but at the time I wasn't good at listening to my body.

I didn't say anything to Hef, or ask his permission. I just did it. I was this brown-haired, bare-faced girl now, in the body I hadn't had since I was eighteen.

I wore sweatshirts. I slept. I took care of myself. I dropped the constant effort, the mask I'd been holding up to my face for eight years. I was too sick—I had no choice. My body made the choice for me. In the back of my mind, I was waiting for the other shoe to drop, for the old Hef to show up one day and give me his disapproving look, point at his own hair and frown critically, tell me to go back to my room and change. But he never did. If he noted the changes, he never said a word.

I wasn't afraid of him anymore.

And he needed me more than ever.

He didn't seem to notice or care that I was sick and needed help, which made me sad. But he also didn't seem to notice or care about the superficial physical things that had always been so important to him. At long last, he accepted me as I was. Or maybe he only saw what he wanted to see, and never noticed that I had shed all my Playmate trappings.

One day, when my iron levels were back to normal and I was bursting with newly appreciated energy, I drove to Disneyland to meet my makeup artist, a guy I'd grown close to and whom I felt I could actually trust. He was gay, but Hef still saw him as a threat. He didn't believe women could be friends with men, even gay men. We walked around the park, talking, eating ice cream. He'd brought a friend along, a guy named Diego. He was a struggling jazz singer and was refreshingly honest about his life in a way that most people in L.A. never are. He seemed real. There was nothing fake about him. He was open, kind, and a good listener. He asked me questions about myself, my past, my interests, and my hopes for the future. It was so unusual to me to talk to someone in this way, especially a man. And unlike Jordan, I could tell it was genuine interest. I didn't have any of the Jordan alarm bells going off. Usually, everyone just wanted something from me. Money, sex, whatever. Diego had no agenda. He just liked me. I couldn't remember the last time I'd had that.

We became friends quickly. And then . . . we became more than friends.

I didn't know if I was in love with him. But I loved being with him. He never wanted anything from me except to spend time with me. He made me feel I was valuable, just for being me. He could say, "It doesn't matter to me what you look like," and I believed him. He thought there was beauty in getting old, and in the physical changes that accompanied it. He thought every phase of life was precious.

He reminded me of Greg a bit. Not in his looks, but in how he made me feel—beautiful for no particular reason. I was sick and weak and struggling to regain my health, but at the same time I also felt like me again. I felt beautiful again.

Being with Diego felt like oxygen after being underwater for a million years. My head broke the surface of the water. I could take a deep, wonderful breath of fresh air.

Then, back to the mansion, where Hef would be waiting for me, looking at the clock.

If I was a minute late he still screamed at the staff. If anything, he was even more possessive now that we were married, now that he depended on me, but it also didn't seem so dire.

The way I felt about Hef in the last few years of our marriage was complicated. It's so hard to pick it apart. I cared for him as a human being. I wanted him to care for me, for that love to be reciprocated, but it always felt shallow. Like when it came to caring for others, he could only reach so far. I still felt hurt that he'd used me in the ways that he had over the years. Now, he told me how much he loved me. How he'd "saved the best for last."

I think he did love me—as much as it was possible for him to love anyone.

At this point, our only intimacy was when I held his hand or kissed his cheek. I was a full-time companion now, his caretaker in every way; guardian of his health, his image, his legacy. Our relationship was about me being there when he needed me, which was just about always. I was at his side for every event. Every photo. Loyal. Present. The supportive, loving wife in public; the nurse carrying his bedpan at night. I still felt deeply indebted to him, programmed to only see what I had been given. I still was not ready to face the truth of everything he'd taken away.

I was still in my twenties, but I had the health of someone six decades older.

Maybe Hef and I were destined to die of old age together.

CHAPTER 16

The Man Behind the Curtain

Hef really wasn't doing well. He was starting to have a tough time with everyday things. He was shaky. He needed help eating his meals, help to get to the bathroom. He was wobbly on his feet and had trouble with his balance. He was visibly frail.

Mary died, in the same way she lived, with attitude and sass, and bossing people from her hospital bed. Hef was sad, but his reaction was muted, even for him. That made me worry even more.

We stuck to the schedule as much as possible. Parties. Movie nights. There was no more leaving the mansion at all, but people still poured into it during the week. We always got a fair number of gawkers—people who'd come for a movie screening and then "get lost" on the way to the bathroom. Security would find people wandering around taking pictures of the worn and dated furniture, the ornate wood paneling in the bathrooms, the old rotary phones built into the walls, the peacocks, the grotto. Guests always wanted to go see the grotto, infamous for its long-ago orgies, scandals, and secrets. But they were usually let down when they saw it. Time had moved on; all that was left out there were some dingy cushions, bottles of baby oil and Coppertone, and empty glasses left by the last party guests who just had to go out there and check it out.

One night, at the end of a crowded movie night, after he'd given a benevolent, grandiose wave and departed the party, Hef fell on the stairs. Hard. Security rushed to his side, lifted him back up. All the guests, milling around in the main hall with their drinks, went quiet. Everybody saw. Everybody stared.

The next time, we had him sit in a chair, and four burly security guys carried him up the stairs while he waved good night. That was better: He seemed like a king being carried on a throne, instead of an old man struggling to get to his bed. I didn't want anyone to see that he was frail, that he could barely walk. He wanted to be the eternal, virile Hugh Hefner, and I wanted that, too. This whole place was built on that image.

I suggested that he try using a walker—I thought maybe I could find a cool one, something with a little elegance, like wooden canes could sometimes have. But he refused.

"Thanks for thinking of me, but no," he said, condescending and dismissive. "It's not for me."

I went out anyway to find one. I walked down the aisles at Walgreens after Walgreens, looking for something that wasn't that depressing, medical-equipment shade of beige, something that didn't look like the handrails on a public toilet stall. Everything was so ugly and embarrassing. I was shocked that there were so few options for older people. There should have been better supplies for illness, disability, and end of life—things that had a little grace and dignity, some beauty, even.

I brought home the least offensive one I could find—it was black and had handbrakes and a little basket in the front that I thought he could use for his scrapbooking supplies and his Pepsi, which he carried with him everywhere. I set it in the corner of the bedroom and didn't say a word about it.

A few days later, I saw him up and out of bed, testing it out, squeezing the hand brakes and leaning on it. Next he was cruising around the mansion with it, Pepsi tucked into the basket along with the Saturday printouts of every mention of his name.

He started talking about death more. It was on his mind.

He wanted to make sure I knew his wishes: to be buried in the crypt he'd bought next to Marilyn, to have a funeral procession to the cemetery, to have all of it documented for the scrapbooks. It was very important to him that everything go in the scrapbook, even after he was dead. But other than that, he had no opinions about how the funeral should go.

"Do whatever you want," he told me. "I won't be there." This giving up of control over what would be his final party was out of character, but then I realized that because he wouldn't be there to see which celebrity showed up, who cried over him, and hear how he was eulogized, he didn't care. And it felt perfectly in character.

I didn't really want to talk about his funeral—I'd had enough death in my life, enough loss. I felt trapped in the mansion, trapped in my role as caretaker, but I also didn't want to lose him. His had been an enormous, outsize presence in my life. He loomed over everything. It was hard to imagine my life without him.

It was safe inside this gilded cage, and because I no longer had to perform in the bedroom, it was easier. I could follow all the rules, and if anything, they only got stricter as he got more frail and needed me in new ways.

He wanted to make sure I was going to be okay when

he was gone. The legalities surrounding his enormous fortune were byzantine, and everything was ultimately controlled by the foundation, wrapped up in *Playboy* stock, and also subject to a postnuptial agreement from his first marriage. The prenuptial agreement I'd signed had stripped me of any claim to his millions, which would go to his children. But he managed to set aside one of his smaller accounts for me, his *Playboy* retirement fund. And he bought a house and put both of our names on the deed, so that I would have a place to go. The mansion had already been sold, with a clause that he could live out his years here. Of course, there was no such clause for me. When the deal was being negotiated with the buyer, a billionaire with a *Playboy* fetish, the office staff pulled me aside and asked me how long I would need to move out after Hef died. "The sooner, the better," they said. We settled on three months to move an entire lifetime and legacy out of the *Playboy* mansion. My stuff would be easy.

I don't know why he fought so hard at the very end of his life to leave me something. Maybe he was trying to buy my time, to keep me at his side—he'd always wanted a happy ending, in his mansion, surrounded by his legacy, with his beautiful bride. Maybe he figured, she didn't cut and run like the other girls, she deserves it. Maybe it was a transaction to him, like so much was: I'd put in the time, and now he was cutting a paycheck. Maybe it was because I didn't ask for it. Everyone else was always asking him for stuff: for money, for cars, for favors. Once, he caught me looking at an ad on my phone, a photo of the Cartier Love bracelet. "Do you want that?" he'd said quickly. "You never ask me for anything. I'll get it for you."

Or maybe he really loved me in some small way.

In the only way he knew how.

My feelings for him had always been complicated, but as I watched even the legendary Hugh Hefner succumb to inevitable aging, I only wanted to give him more of what he needed from me as he struggled to walk, to stand, to eat, and manage his business. I offered him more comfort, more attention, more care and love than he had ever shown to anyone. The staff was there, of course, but they were just doing their jobs, and in the end, he was a paycheck to them and to some just a way to be famous-adjacent.

There were some staff, of course, who genuinely loved him and who were loyal to him for decades. Apart from a few, he rarely knew their names.

I became hyper-vigilant about protecting his image. I had been oppressed by this man who was so invested in being "the man," but in his later years I worked hard to keep up his myth. I propped him up physically, emotionally, and reputationally.

I was never in love with Hef, but I loved this old man in the ways you are supposed to love your elders. In the ways you are supposed to love someone who is nearing the end of a long and complicated life. I put every resentment aside, because legally I was his wife, and it was my duty to care for him.

Yes, I had been heavily programmed to believe I would be nothing without him, so if I paused during those last two years to reflect I may have seen my mounting panic at what I would do and who I would be when he was gone. But I didn't stop to consider all the ways I had volunteered for my own captivity—all the ways I had walked into a life that was so stifling of who I was inside. We all make tradeoffs, compromises, and we settle for less than we might need or want or even deserve when it comes to relationships. My entire twenties were spent under the control of a person, an institution, and a myth, that was so much bigger than

I had in me to push against. Crystal Harris didn't know how to stand up for herself. And Crystal Hefner didn't know herself well enough to know what she really wanted or needed to fight for.

In August of that year, I went on vacation—my first real vacation in ten years. No Hef, no paid appearances, no cameras, no paparazzi, no work events, no expectations of any kind other than rest and relaxation

I didn't ask Hef if I could go, because if I did, the answer would be no. I just told him.

"I'm going on a trip," I said. "I will be back in one week."

He didn't want me to go, and that's something I have to live with. "Go when I'm gone," he said. But in my mind he would never be gone. I didn't want him to be gone. But I did want a break from my caregiving. I needed to be far away.

I went to the Cook Islands, a string of tiny islands out in the middle of the vast Pacific. I wanted to feel like nobody could reach me. I lay in the sun. I floated in the endless blue water. I went with Diego, and it was romantic, and sexy, and fun, and adventurous. Diego made me feel young again. He made me feel hopeful again.

I couldn't remember a time in my life since my dad died that I had actually felt so carefree. In those islands I laughed and I played and I spent hours daydreaming about traveling to magical places in the world. There was so much of the world I had never seen from my little window of the mansion. I tried not to feel guilty about leaving Hef. I tried not to feel guilty about this time that was just for me.

When I came home, something was wrong.

"He doesn't want to go down to movie night," said Wyatt. I had hired Wyatt against Hef's wishes, just like I'd brought in the walker. He'd been insistent: *no nurse*. But Wyatt was a man, big and burly, and he was a vet. He had a knack with Hef, and he was gentle with his self-image. Hef loved him.

Hef had never missed a movie night. Not once. But he refused to get out of bed. We even had a shiny new elevator that had just been installed—he'd only used it one time so far—but he wouldn't be coaxed. He was totally indifferent.

He wanted us to proceed with the regular mansion schedule, so we did. I kept rushing downstairs to make appearances, reassure the guests that Hef was just a little under the weather, that he was resting. But everyone knew something was off. It was so out of the ordinary. Hef had always, his entire life, wanted to be the life of every party, at the center of the action.

And then Jennifer came rushing out of the office with some pages she'd printed off the Internet.

"I think he might have a urinary tract infection," she said. "Look, look at the symptoms: It says aloof, checked out, confused."

She was right. Hef's doctor took a sample and ran a panel. The news was bad. He did indeed have a UTI, but it was an extremely aggressive bacteria, a strain of E. coli that was considered a "superbug"—highly resistant to antibiotics and difficult to treat. Hef's doctor knew of only one drug that could target it, but it was some obscure antibiotic that the hospital didn't have. Desperate, I called my own doctor, who'd been treating me for Lyme disease— miraculously, she had it. It was the weekend, but she rounded up one of her nurses and came over.

Rapidly, we turned the master bedroom into a hospital room. Monitors, an IV stand, everything you'd have in the ER intensive care unit to treat someone who was fighting this kind of superbug. The only thing we did not change was the bed. Hef hated hospitals—he said that hospitals were where people go to die. He hated the thought of a hospital so much, he refused to ever have white sheets on his bed. So his bed was made the same as it always had been: in black silk.

When the nurse, Mario, started the bag of IV fluids, I sat and held Hef's hand. He absolutely hated needles. I explained to him that it was all to help him, that he would feel better once the fluids got going, and that it would be over in just a second.

Mario slipped the needle in, and Hef squeezed my hand.

I squeezed back.

"Are you okay?" I asked him.

"I'm okay," he said, sounding defeated. And he closed his eyes.

Those were his last words.

The next day, he drifted in and out of consciousness, but he did not speak again. He wouldn't eat or drink. The doctor said he was entering sepsis, and that the antibiotics weren't working. He was too old, too frail; the superbug was too strong. There was fluid building up in his lungs.

I called his daughter and told her to come. I called all his doctors and told them to come. I called his lawyer, who could decipher his wishes on the health directive. The house filled with nurses and specialists and people frantically trying to help. I was in a state of panic.

And I did not want him to know. I wasn't sure how much he was aware of, but I remembered my dad, being in that awful fluorescent hospital room with the beeping machines and alarms, with everyone talking about how he was dying right in front of him. Crying and fighting right in front of him. Being told to say, "It's okay to go," which I had regretted my entire life. I didn't think it was my place to ever tell someone that it was their time to die—or to tell my dad it was okay to go. It wasn't okay for him to go. It had never been okay for him to go. I had never been okay since my dad had gone.

I didn't want Hef to experience any of that. I would not stand for it.

I didn't want him to know that he was dying.

I didn't want him to know that Hugh Hefner, in the end, was just an old man in a bed, dying.

I sent people out of the room if they said one negative word. If the doctors wanted to discuss his care, they had to step out.

I pushed people around, I stood my ground, and I protected him. Taking care of Hef in those final days, I was the strongest and most assertive I had ever been in that home.

I put *The Wizard of Oz* up on the big televisions, on a loop. It's such a visual movie, with the bright Technicolor and the easy-to-follow story; I thought, if he woke up he could just look at it, and he might enjoy the songs. *Somewhere over the rainbow...* My dad used to sing that song. I hoped it would be soothing for him, if he somehow knew what was happening to him, to hear those familiar lyrics. I knew the magical world of Oz would be a comfort to him as he left his own magical world.

I sat by his side, scrolling through medical articles on my phone, searching for an answer the doctors hadn't found yet. At the end, when the huge imposing face of Oz dissolves, and they whip the curtain open, I looked up and watched. I thought about how Hef really had been the man behind the curtain all these years. He'd seemed all-powerful, eternal, and indestructible.

But he was just a man, pretending to be a wizard.

There was no clarity from anyone on his wishes. He'd put me in charge of the paperwork. I was supposed to decide what to do. But nobody could tell me what was right. If we took him to the hospital, there was maybe a 30 percent chance he could be saved. But what if we took him, and he suffered, and then he died anyway? The medical team assured me there wasn't any more a hospital could do than what they were doing here at home, but then said he needed a feeding tube put in, which would require a hospital bed. All these medical professionals—nurses, doctors, kidney specialists—looked to me to make this decision. His life was in my hands, and I felt unprepared for the responsibility.

I pulled everyone out of the room.

The doctor, the lawyer, Jennifer, and I all stood in the hall, outside his closed door, poring over the health directive, trying to figure out what he would want me to do—take him to the hospital? Don't take him to the hospital? He had a do not resuscitate order if he was terminally ill, but I still didn't know if this infection counted as a terminal illness. What if the hospital could save him? Did he want to be saved, at this point? What sorts of measures did he want us to take? If it was going to be painful, should we just let him go? I was crying so hard I couldn't read the document through the blur of tears.

I didn't want to give up. I thought, *Maybe if we try another antibiotic...* I asked the doctor about the medicines I had been researching online. There had to be something we hadn't tried. Some new medicine, some new treatment, something, anything...

While we were in the middle of debating, one of the nurses came out of the bedroom and said simply, quietly, "He's gone."

I rushed back into the room and to Hef's side, and I knew the nurse was right. Hef was gone. I already knew, from watching my father's death, how hard it is to watch someone die—to witness that moment, so quick and small, but at the same time so enormous, so permanent. Last time I ran out; this time I ran in.

This time I stayed.

I can't remember what time of day it was. We'd been inside, with the drapes closed, with the movie flickering its bright colors in the background, for so long. And when the medical team tried to read out the time for the nurse to record, I cut him off.

"I don't want to know," I said. "I don't want to know what time it is, I don't want to know what day it is."

A nurse shut Hef's eyes and wrapped a soft piece of cloth, gently, around his jaw, to keep his mouth closed.

Christie, his daughter, hadn't made it to the mansion yet. A part of me thought she was going to blame me for Hef dying before she could get there. A part of me thought the world was going to blame me for Hef dying.

Christie was still en route, traveling from Chicago, and she had made it clear she wanted to see him one last time in the mansion, where she'd always visited him. So I sent everyone away and told them to leave him there, in his bed, until Christie could see him and say her goodbyes.

I didn't want to lie in bed next to him—it felt like lying in a grave. But I didn't want him to be alone. There was nothing he hated more than being alone.

So I lay on the floor, until four a.m., when Christie finally arrived. She came in and leaned over him; she said some words softly. I wondered what she was feeling. We had never been close, and I didn't know her well, but I thought he was probably a hard person to have had as a father. I thought of saying goodbye to my own father, and my heart went out to her.

When she was done saying goodbye the mortuary came, and in the early morning hours while the dew gathered on the great lawn, the mansion gates swung open for Hugh Hefner one last time, and they took him away.

CHAPTER 17

Aftermath

When Hef's death was announced they said he died of natural causes, surrounded by family. It wasn't exactly true: He wasn't surrounded by family when he passed, but it made his death sound nicer. Easier. After that official statement, his son, Cooper, released a statement:

> "My father lived an exceptional and impactful life as a media and cultural pioneer and a leading voice behind some of the most significant social and cultural movements of our time in advocating free speech, civil rights and sexual freedom. He defined a lifestyle and ethos that lie at the heart of the *Playboy* brand, one of the most recognizable and enduring in history. He will be greatly missed by many, including his wife Crystal, my sister Christie and my brothers David and Marston, and all of us at Playboy Enterprises."

The statement made me sad. It sounded corporate, on brand, but there was nothing from a son to a father in it. There was no heart, but I guess that was also on brand.

I couldn't stay in the bedroom where he had died. It never

felt like my bedroom anyway, or even "our" bedroom, as most married couples might say. It was his. Not once did I ever feel like I could lounge in bed or have a lazy day reading or watching television. I had been through so much in that bed, and now Hef had died in that bed. I didn't want to see that bed ever again.

I moved into Bedroom 4, which the staff sometimes called "The Cloud Room," because there were clouds painted on the ceiling. I lay in there, looking up at the fake sky, thinking of all the things we could have done differently with his passing. I ruminated on whether we could have saved him, prolonged his life. I was angry that we hadn't done more—we should have tried more antibiotics, all the antibiotics; there were three that might have worked, why hadn't we just done all three at once? When I'd been treated for Lyme disease, they'd given me six at once. I was consumed with doubt and regret, and kept going over every little decision we'd made, imagining that if we'd chosen differently, he would still be here.

Paparazzi descended on the mansion; flowers started piling up at the back gate. The family decided to go out to dinner at Katsuya, a Hollywood hot spot, but it was a mecca for paparazzi, and that's the last thing I wanted to do.

When Hef's death was announced, the tributes started filling social media from celebrities, actors, former Playmates, social justice leaders like Jesse Jackson. Kendra tweeted:

> Can't really put in to words how I really feel. It's easy to say he will be missed and how much I loved him. There's a lot more than that.

It seemed like a beautiful post on its surface, and people immediately offered their condolences. But the post landed differently to me. I could relate to her use of the passive voice, and to everything she was saying by not really saying anything directly. She didn't say she would miss him. She didn't say she loved him. She didn't say how she really felt.

I got it.

It was complicated.

I read all the tributes as they came in, hiding in the cloud room on my phone. The *New York Times* ran an obituary and recapped my runaway bride status and my return. I realized all these media outlets had his obituary ready to print long before he actually passed away. It felt wrong somehow, to be so ready for someone's death.

There was backlash when the president of GLAAD criticized the media for their praise. She wrote:

"It's alarming how media is attempting to paint Hugh Hefner as a pioneer or social justice activist, because nothing could be further from reality. Hefner was not a visionary. He was a misogynist who built an empire on sexualizing women and mainstreaming stereotypes that caused irreparable damage to women's rights and our entire culture."

I read her last sentence over and over again. She had said the secret thing out loud, and I was shocked. My nervous system went on alert, waiting for all hell to break loose in the mansion and for Hef to go on one of his infamous tirades when things did not go his way, but there was only silence. The number one rule of Hef's world is you didn't say anything bad about Hef. Life was a classic Hollywood romance, and life was good. That was the party line, but it hit me that the party was over.

I should have felt relieved, but I only felt afraid.

I was expected to make an official statement, but nobody actually asked me how I felt. I had promised him over and over again that I would only say good things, and that's what I did when I released my own statement expressing my disbelief and my heartbreak.

But as with Kendra there was subtext to my words.

I thought of the miners I had watched on television years ago emerging from a cave collapse they had been trapped in, their eyes blinking at the sudden light of day, the overwhelm at the crowd and press of people, the shock of freedom after what was most likely a dark acceptance of their fate.

It wasn't the same at all, but I imagined them asking themselves the same question I was: "What happens now?" When you've been living so long in a weird and dark world, how do you transition back to the light?

Everybody kept coming to me with questions. There were people knocking at the door all day, or swooping in as soon as I came out, asking urgently: What should the gravestone say? How should his name read on the stone? Which urn should his ashes be placed in? I couldn't believe they were coming to me as though I was in charge—*Why are you asking me?* I kept wanting to say, before I realized: I'm his next of kin. I'm his wife. I'm his widow.

It's my job to decide.

I chose an urn that reminded me of the mansion itself: It was ornately carved, dark, glossy wood. There was a lock and a key, which gave it a sense of exclusivity, of locking people out who might want to come in. I thought he would like that.

The funeral was tiny: just me, my mom, Jennifer, his head of security, his doctor, and Hef's kids. There was a white privacy tent set up over the crypt, so that we could bury him without being observed and photographed. After the short service, everyone filed out quickly to let me have the last moments with him. My mom stood right outside the tent door, hovering.

Once I was alone, I lost my composure.

I kissed the side of his glossy urn once; it was hard and cold. And then I started sobbing. I cried for Hef, and I grieved for all the mistakes we had made. I cried for the small man under the big myth, who needed so desperately to be propped up by everyone around him. I had never been able to visit Greg's tombstone after his death, so I cried for Greg. I cried for a boy I once loved and who once loved me. I cried for the sweetness of that love, the simplicity of it, and the lost potential. What if Greg hadn't died and we had gotten married? Maybe I'd have had a home full of laughter and joy and play and a real relationship with someone who loved even the parts of me that were quiet and shy. Maybe I would have had a child already, someone to love and protect and comfort.

I kneeled in the dirt and cried for my dad because I still missed him, and his death had made all deaths hard for me. All relationships are hard for me. I cried because, even with my mom hovering outside, I felt abandoned and alone.

Again.

Still.

I cried for the girl who had excitedly walked up the mansion steps, sure that every beautiful, shiny thing she saw in that house was made of real gold. I was thirty-one years old, and I felt more lost than I'd been before I walked through the mansion doors at twenty-one. I'd spent ten years molding myself to fit into the twisted world of a powerful man.

And that powerful man was gone. Nothing more than ashes in a cold urn.

This life was ending, and I cried because I had no idea what to do, where to go, or how to be.

I cried because I had no idea who I was.

I stayed closed up at the mansion for six weeks after Hef's death. I knew they were all waiting for me to leave. Somewhere was that billionaire, waiting to claim his prize, the Playboy Mansion. I said I was packing, but there was very little of my own to pack. This house did not belong to me; almost nothing in it did. But I was terrified to leave.

Diego called and texted, but I didn't pick up. I couldn't.

I had spent so much of the past ten years wanting to be out of this house every second I could be, speeding home for curfew, only to wake up and get out just as fast as I could. But now that I was free to go, I couldn't leave. I couldn't see what my life looked like on the other side of the gates.

I didn't know where I belonged, if I didn't belong to a powerful man.

So I stayed in the house for as long as I could, and watched as the mansion staff took the place apart, bit by bit.

The three thousand scrapbooks went to Iron Mountain, an exclusive, expensive, and secure storage facility for corporations and the rich and famous. The original paintings that I had been so in awe of my first night—the Picasso, the Jackson Pollock— weren't actually real, but were still packed with care as if they were priceless artworks. I don't know where they went, perhaps to one of Hef's kids or maybe sold off. All of Hef's memorabilia was whisked away. Things disappeared. The mansion was dismantled before my eyes.

I knew I had to go somewhere. I couldn't go to the house he'd bought in my name—it was big and empty, and the address was public—photographers had been staking it out, and people were leaving things for me there. I didn't want to be watched, to be under the microscope, my every movement analyzed and judged. And I didn't want to be alone in a big, empty, impersonal house.

The houses I had invested in were either rented or already sold, so I found a tiny little 600-square-foot bungalow and bought it with my own money. I felt safe there. It was high in the hills, tiny, with a view that made you feel you could see anything coming your way. It was like a nest, where nobody could reach me.

I left the mansion under the cover of night. It seemed fitting.

I'd spent the day packing some more things for storage, gathering my last few belongings together, finalizing paperwork with the office staff, and saying goodbye. The staff at the mansion had been the closest I had to friends all these years. It was hard to say goodbye.

When I went out to get in my car, it was dark. I started the car and shifted to drive and then realized—after ten years of racing home for curfew, of racing home before dark, I had no idea how to turn the headlights on. *In my own car.*

I fumbled around in the darkness, sweeping my hand behind the steering column, flipping buttons. The windshield wipers went on, then the back wipers. And then *whoosh,* the headlights blinked on. And there was the road, curving away from the mansion, where it always had been.

I drove away.

Things with Diego quickly fell apart. Maybe if I'd met him at another time, it might have worked out. But it had overlapped too much with the mansion. It had happened in secret, in whatever pockets of time I could find before curfew and in between my responsibilities to Hef. And it carried the stain of a secret. Of my guilt over Hef's death.

We could never lift it.

I hid in my bungalow nest. I saw very few people. I saw only the people who had been in my life for a very long time, whom I knew I could trust: like Noah, a friend from pre-mansion times. He wasn't comfortable at the mansion, and Hef didn't approve of me having a male best friend, so we hadn't spent much time together over the last ten years. Noah was like a brother to me; he had always been a steady friend. His face at my door was a relief.

One night, as we sat talking, I said, "I wonder what would have happened to me if I'd never gone into the mansion. What my life would have been."

"Oh, you'd have figured it out," he said. "You were always destined for something big."

It was a sweet thing to say. But I didn't have his confidence.

Confidence. It was something I had never had—ever.

What would have had to go differently in my life for me to not have been so desperate to walk into the world of *Playboy*? Was there something in my DNA that made me vulnerable to its dark allure? I thought about everything in the world that told me I was only valued because of my looks, that pushed me to be sexually available, and then punished me for being sexually available. Where did I learn that beauty is a tool to get ahead, and men hold all the power?

How far back would I have had to go, to change my trajectory? To my dad's death? Earlier? Before he died, things had been different. Better. He'd been a force for calm and creativity, but all of that vanished with him. But had I been safer from all those dark forces? I remember that my parents were always dragging me around to shows—my dad would play, and then they'd want to stay and party. I fell asleep in those smoky bars, on a booth somewhere in the back, while they danced, arms around each other, beer bottles in hand. I grew up listening to their conversations about wanting more out of life, wanting less struggle for their children; their dreams of fame and fortune and bright Hollywood lights were fed to me like vitamins.

My dad made me feel loved. He was always dreaming, thinking, inventing—one of his inventions was a "six in one" shopping cart that turned into a clothes hanger and a laundry cart, like a Transformer; another idea he had was a bracelet you wore on your wrist while surfing, that would release a big flotation balloon to save you if you got into trouble in the water. That's what it felt like to have my dad around—a balloon that will keep you afloat in a rough sea. But even he could not protect me from everything. And his death made all the seas around me rougher.

All of that was just history now. What happened, happened. My parents were who they were and wanted what they wanted. I couldn't blame them for that. My dad had died, and life had gone the way it did. I couldn't know if it wouldn't have been hard in other ways. Greg would have still died. I probably still would have tried to be a model, attaching all my value to what I looked like, to who was willing to love me.

Noah cleared his throat, interrupting my reverie. He was used to me going silent for long periods. Hef's death had left me perpetually in shock, spaced out, and unsure.

"If you didn't go to the party at the mansion, you would have finished out the semester and graduated college. You'd probably be a famous psychologist now helping people with all their problems."

I looked at him, and we both were silent, until we burst into laughter.

It was the first time I had laughed since Hef's death, and that little bit of laughter, even if it was at my own expense, felt good.

It felt like hope, and it sounded like freedom.

And maybe I would help people someday, but right now, I had to figure out a way to help myself.

CHAPTER 18

The Inner Voice

I was free of the mansion, but it wasn't as if I could suddenly just be myself. I still had obligations to Hef and to *Playboy*.

I still had a job to do.

Since Hef's death, I'd been on the board of the Hugh Hefner Foundation, as Hef had wanted. It had been my job to carry the torch, and so I had been, posting tributes to Hef on his birthday, and on our anniversary, on the day he died. On the second anniversary of his death, Jennifer wrote a post for me to send out. This is what she said as me:

Hef passed away on September 27, 2017. On the 2nd anniversary of his death, we remember his love of life, his infectious laugh, and his lifelong fight against injustice. We celebrate him as a true visionary, an activist, adventurer, and coolest pajama wearer. We miss you, Hef.

I'd tried hard to always say the things that he would have wanted me to say. But I'd been glossing over a lot. It was all gloss. I hadn't wanted to let anybody down, not Hef, and not his family. At the memorial for Hef that we had at the mansion after his funeral, Christie had gotten up and talked about what a positive presence I'd been, and I felt compelled to keep being that for all of them. "When Crystal came into his life—" she'd begun, and then burst into tears.

I felt this heavy responsibility to all of them, to keep being that person: loyal, supportive, unflagging. But the more distance I got from the mansion, the stranger that whole world, that whole part of my life, seemed. Was it even real? Was that even me? I'd done so many things I shouldn't have. I'd been through things that nobody should have to go through. The more time that passed, the more I realized how much it had messed with me—with my self-worth, my confidence, my ability to have normal relationships in life.

I was having to relearn who I was. What friendships were. What love was.

I should have been angry, and sometimes I was. But I also felt sad for him. He created this world that brought to life his wildest dreams, but it was empty. He never felt fulfilled. It was never enough. He wanted to live this *Playboy* life, and be the alpha male and the gentleman with the smoking jacket, an important person who would go down in history. But he was a lost soul himself, and his legacy was breaking apart as the truth came out.

Only say good things. I still felt I owed him that much—to keep that promise.

But it was getting harder and harder to do.

I felt the gap growing between who I was online and in the press and who I was really. I was still performing. It was exhausting, and it wasn't true. I didn't want to participate anymore in this image machine. Maybe it was possible to talk about the good *and* the bad of my experiences, to be more honest. Sure—Hef had done some good things in his life. But he'd done a lot of damage, too. And I was some of that collateral damage.

The mansion itself hadn't been the prison, even though I'd thought it was.

The prison was everywhere.

The images on social media, of impossible-to-attain physical perfection. In the media. In movies. In the pages of every magazine. The women walking around L.A. with their surgically perfected bodies. I felt like I could not escape the relentless message that *you are what you look like.* When I posted online, the photos where I wore less clothing got more likes—hundreds of thousands more. And it felt good to see those little hearts clicked. The more notifications I had, the more of an endorphin rush I felt.

Oh no, I thought. *I'm doing it again.* But like an addiction, I could not stop.

Hef could be so shallow. Everything he valued was skin-deep. That world made me shallow, too. I'd forgotten how to look past the surface, how to go deeper, to where real connection happened. Losing Greg had made me realize just how painful deep connections were when they were gone. So had losing my dad. Maybe the trauma of those two losses had already primed me to live in a world that was only surface level before I got to the mansion. Either way, I was susceptible.

I was the kind of broken and lost that the Playboy Mansion welcomed with open arms. I bought in because I had nothing else to buy into.

When I met someone new, I found myself saying, "I really like him—he's so hot."

We dated for a while, this new guy and I, but toward the end he said to me, "I think if I stopped working out, you wouldn't like me."

I insisted that it wasn't true—but it was truer than I wanted to admit. I was just as guilty of judging others based on their appearance.

For so long, my job had been to be physically perfect and match a certain ideal. Slipping would have meant losing everything. And while I knew now what I wanted—to live a life where my value was not entirely based on my appearance—I didn't know how to do that.

When I looked in the mirror, I found so many flaws. It was harder since my breast implant removal. I'd had no choice—they were breaking down, leaking toxins into my body, and slowly killing me—but I was so unhappy with how I looked. And I fell for a new procedure I'd heard about: fat transfer surgery. They took fat from one part of your body and moved it into your breasts. I rationalized that it was all-natural, since it was *my* fat, so it wasn't so bad to do.

I almost died on the operating table.

Something went horribly wrong as they were finishing up, and I started bleeding out. I lost half the blood in my body.

I was rushed to the hospital. I remember feeling cold and shaky. I struggled to understand what was happening, but I knew it was bad. I had this fleeting thought: that I might die because I couldn't unlearn these terrible lessons.

It was a breaking point.

For so long, I'd been pushing down my inner voice, that instinct that was trying to scream at me that things weren't right, that I wasn't okay. I slammed the door on her. I thought she would talk me out of opportunity and success, and that I would regret passing them up. She was trying to save me, but I didn't see it. I think I silenced her so much that she went quiet. I lost track of who I was and what I wanted. To this day, I have to work very hard to hear her. But I get glimpses here and there. I know she's my compass, and I'm doing my best to make her voice louder.

I am still struggling with the powerful instinct to "be what they want." It is so ingrained in me.

I went down that road, looking for love, acceptance, and success. I lived in that house. And I lost far too much.

After the mansion, I dated a few men who pursued me for who I'd been in my *Playboy* days. But it didn't feel right. And this time I listened to that whisper that said, *Get out*. I didn't want to do it all again—get lost in somebody else's world, follow somebody else's rules, prop up someone's ego at my own expense, be somebody else's idea of what a woman should be. I finally decided: I was done with all that.

Never again.

When the #metoo movement swept through social media, I scrolled through every post, hungry for the stories and the hope of recovery, of a better future. I felt so validated. I felt the shame melting away, for the things I'd done because I was backed into a corner, because it seemed like the only way forward. I felt more at peace with having such conflicting emotions surrounding my time in Hef's world. So much of my intuition had told me, *This is not good. This is not okay.* But I'd ignored it, second-guessed it. I never trusted that inner voice. But she'd been right the whole time.

I put on a movie now, and if it has that toxic male gaze, I turn it off. It makes me angry. I don't want to see the world through that lens anymore, where they decide who's beautiful, who's valuable, who's worth their time.

I sometimes feel these waves of regret: *What was it all for?* I gave a decade of my life to that place. I lost my sense of self. I lost my compass. And for what? The legacy is crumbling. We've all seen what the Playboy Mansion is really, and what it always was: a fading relic falling into disrepair, a promise of sexual liberation that was always a lie, a glamorous mirage that turned out to be a trap.

But I am who I am because of my experiences—good and bad.

I was invited to a polo party in upstate New York, and I didn't want to go. My social anxiety, a side effect from being in the mansion and in the public eye, was in full bloom. Yes, I had been in *Playboy* twice, but at my core I was more shy than not. But I went anyway because I had sealed myself off for so long, I was craving connection. And right away, the host took me by the elbow and steered me over to this woman. My age, pretty, with a genuine smile. He introduced us—*Crystal this is Anne; Anne, Crystal*—and then vanished into the crowd.

We started chatting—and it just felt so natural. It felt like we were already friends. I was startled to feel that way about another woman—there was no model for genuine female friendship at the mansion—so meeting Anne and connecting right away felt revelatory. Hef would have hated it. I hadn't had a real female friend in years. Decades. But now Anne was telling me about her childhood, about being adopted; I started talking about Hef, and how I'd ended up at the mansion, like a kid who went trick or treating somewhere and never left.

All of a sudden, the two of us were in the back of a golf cart, leaning on each other and crying.

We are friends to this day. Anne is very trusting—she'll trust people far past the point she should. And I don't trust anyone anymore. We keep each other in check. I remind her that you have to check in with your instincts. She reminds me to be more open, that there's a lot of good in the world. Amber and I are still friends, and sometimes I call her just to say, "I just remembered . . . did that really happen?" I can tell Anne stories, and she is understanding and listens deeply, but only someone who lived what I lived really understands.

I am slowly building more friendships with women and learning how much more power there is in having a close circle of women around you. Not naked in a bed covered in whipped cream and posing for a camera, but women who have your back. Who cheer for your successes and commiserate with your setbacks. Women who share opportunities and want to collaborate rather than compete. I read recently that women live longer, healthier lives the more close female friendships they have, and that makes sense to me now. That's something I wish I had been taught as a young girl, something I wish I had read about in the pages of magazines that only told me how to lose weight and keep a boyfriend.

I didn't go crazy with my freedom outside the mansion. I didn't stay out late or party until dawn just because I could. Instead I traveled. I went to far-off places like Egypt and Dubai and the Maldives and back to England, where I had lived with my parents. I visited Hawaii, where I fell in love with the rain forests and the wild ocean cliffs. I learned I am so much happier in nature than I had ever been at a movie premiere or a party.

Everywhere I went, I learned something new about myself and something new about the world.

When I came back from my travels, I started looking for a house to move into more permanently—a real home. I'd lived as a guest for a decade, and I wanted a place that felt like mine. I scoured the city, but so many houses in L.A. just felt like cold, modern boxes. And then I saw photos of a home up on a hill that had something about it that spoke to me: a calmness and serenity. I went to see it, and the place was trashed—it had clearly been someone's party house and needed a lot of work. But you could see the good bones underneath. You could see the potential. And from the patio behind the house, the whole city unfurled like a smoggy, sunset-colored, light-spangled carpet. There was this grassy hill that plunged down into the canyon. I looked down and saw deer picking their way through the tall, dry grass, a mother and two fawns. I felt completely at peace.

And I learned something else I didn't know about myself: that I was someone who wanted peace. I was someone who needed a sanctuary.

In many ways that house was like me: It had been through a lot, but underneath it was solid.

It has become one of my compass points.

At a recent family reunion, my niece pulled a VHS tape out of a box of stuff she'd brought from her mom, my sister's, house. "Ray Harris live performance," she read off the label. "I didn't know him that well, but I've always wanted to see this!"

She popped the tape in. And suddenly, there he was, with his mane of dark hair, singing, sounding just a little raspier than I remember. A memory came back to me: He was supposed to perform that night, but had a sore throat and thought about canceling. But in the end, he went. Ray Harris could never let people down who were counting on him. And they recorded it.

I made it through the first song okay. But for the second number, he sang "Over the Rainbow." And I just lost it.

Alarmed, my niece leaped up to turn it off, but I waved her away and kept watching. My tears were for the good times and for the love he gave me. I was done grieving the loss.

For more than twenty years, I'd kept everything of my dad's hidden away. I couldn't be reminded of what I'd lost. But the other day, I bought a frame and put a picture of him up—a photo from that performance, actually, the one he did when his throat was sore. It's nice to see his face looking back at me when I walk around my house. And I hung his blue guitar over my desk. I want these cues around me, to remind me to be creative, to be bold, and to be myself, unapologetically.

There's no neat ending to this fairy tale, but that's okay. I'm not looking for fairy-tale endings any longer.

I am a work in progress.

And that's more exciting than scary now. I don't have to have it all figured out, and sometimes you only know who you are by what you are not any longer. I am not someone who needs a man to give her strength. I am not defined by my body or my looks.

My worth is not determined by how many people like my bikini picture on social media.

I have no bikini pictures on my social media.

People are always asking me how I "really" felt about Hef. *Did you love him? Did you trust him?*

I'm never really sure how to answer. Yes, I loved him, but I loved him the way someone might love their kidnapper after ten years of being with them every day. I felt sorry for him, that he didn't know how to love, how to actually *see* another person, or how to really connect in a meaningful way.

The man thought to be the greatest lover in the world never knew how to love at all.

In the end, it's just sad.

And trust—that's trickier. Did I trust him in the way you're supposed to trust someone in a marriage, when it's just the two of you, when there's mutual love and respect? No. Absolutely not. That was never possible for me at the Playboy Mansion. But I could count on him. He was like this invincible umbrella I was under. If anything happened, I was protected under this powerful thing. Now, I am my own umbrella. And that's harder, because life can be hard, but it's so much better.

I did a lot of things I didn't feel comfortable doing while I was at the mansion. Countless, endless things. Every time my inner voice tried to scream at me that things weren't okay, I pushed it away, and I refused to listen.

I try not to do that any longer.

I try to listen. I try to make her voice louder and other voices softer. It's not always easy, but I try.

I visited Iron Mountain recently, the room where the three thousand scrapbooks live, each one encased in plastic. I pulled out the pictures from Halloween weekend. It's Volume 2199, October 31–November 5, 2008. The cover picture is Amber and me flanking Hef. We are wearing the dresses we frantically changed into the next day and were wearing as we drove back up to the gates hoping that security would let us back in. My dress is polka-dot, and my hair is in pigtails. I look young and happy. I had just been invited to spend the weekend at the Playboy Mansion after having the wildest night of my life.

I stared at my face. There is no fear or worry. One of the most powerful men in the world has his arm around me, so I feel powerful and beautiful and special. In the picture I am beaming at the camera.

Staring at the picture, I didn't want to yell at my younger self and tell her to run.

I have compassion for her, but I think maybe she needs to go through everything that's to come so she can emerge stronger.

I put the binder back and pulled out random others from my ten years at the mansion. There's one scrapbook with the title:

"Crystal Apologizes to Me." I look through every page, but there's no apology I can find, just articles about my returning to the mansion after our time apart.

In one book I found one of the millions of letters that people wrote to Hef over his ninety-one years. It's from a sixth grade girl named Mackenzie, who writes to Hef that she's eleven years old and watches *The Girls Next Door*. It's her favorite show. "I have a dream to become a playmate," she writes. "It will always be my lifelong dream!"

She said in the letter that on her thirteenth birthday she is going to buy herself a *Playboy* bunny bedspread. "My mom always tells me that she's always going to support me through my dreams."

I can feel the tears start behind my eyes as I keep reading. "Hef, my two big questions are, 'How old do you have to be to come live in the Playboy mansion?' and 'What do you have to do to get in the mansion?' Anyways, I'll always love the mansion and you. I'll love you forever."

There was a picture of her in a school uniform, blond and smiling, her hair sticking up a little in the back, her school tie in a loose knot at the front.

I sat down on the floor and stared at Mackenzie's picture. I didn't cry for the picture of me, but I cried for the picture of Mackenzie. I cried for any part I had in making the mansion Mackenzie's biggest dream, for any way I contributed to inspiring Mackenzie to write this letter. I hope wherever she is, she never found out the answer to her questions to Hef. *What do you have to do to get in the mansion?*

You have to lose yourself, Mackenzie, you have to give up everything about you that makes you unique and special. You have to give up your mind and your opinions and any belief in choosing your own future. But mostly you have to get really, really small. So small you don't leave a trace. So small you don't cast a shadow. So small and so quiet that even if you are screaming you can't hear it.

There are other letters in other scrapbooks, a million little girls sold a lie. There's a letter from a young man thanking Hef for teaching him how to treat women.

I couldn't read any more. I put the scrapbooks away and turned off the lights. When I closed the heavy vault door I knew that I wouldn't come back. I wouldn't pull these books off the shelves again, because they belong in the past, in the darkness. Alone.

When *Playboy* announced Hef's death, they posted a black-and-white picture of him, his hands folded reverently in front of him. At the bottom of the picture they put a quote from him.

"Life is too short to be living somebody else's dream."

I'd heard him say that before, but never to any women. Certainly never to the women he called his girlfriends.

His babies.

His beauties.

He certainly never said it to me, his wife.

But as I walked out of Iron Mountain and started the drive to my new home, I thought it might be the best advice I'd ever heard.

Thank you, Hef.

Life is short, but I'm finally ready to start living my own dream. It's not the big, glamorous dream of fame and fortune I once thought it would be. My dream is simple. Happiness. Friendship. Love. Truth.

The journey to finding myself after leaving the mansion doesn't end, but I'm finally ready to listen to the voice inside me that's been there all along.

That voice gets louder every day.

So, yes, I used to only say good things, but now, I say whatever I want.

ACKNOWLEDGMENTS

There are so many people who've helped me on this journey and I'm grateful for them all. I want to especially thank all my supporters, people who have followed my journey every step of the way, and the fans who have become friends. You have grown alongside me and I love you all.

Lara Love Hardin. Mama Love. I can't even begin to describe what a force you are. This book wouldn't be here if it weren't for you. Your love, time, compassion, and more importantly way of closely relating to me even though the hard things we individually went through were different, will forever be appreciated. I will always follow your lead on never judging anyone or myself based on the worst thing that we have ever done. Thank you for allowing me to finally put my own shame to rest. For helping me set it down with the words on the pages of this book. For lighting the path for me, advocating for me. For all the laughs and light we found along the way of telling a complicated and dark story. You are the best agent in the world. Thank you also to Miles Michelle of True Literary who was invaluable in editing and offering input to our many drafts.

Alyssa Knickerbocker. I started out unsure, and after countless Zoom hours, cried because you helped me finally find my voice on the page. Thank you for listening to my story and helping get my thoughts into words for the book proposal.

ACKNOWLEDGMENTS

I want to thank Hachette Book Group and the entire team at Grand Central Publishing, especially my editor, Suzanne O'Neill. Thank you for championing my story and editing each draft so brilliantly. Thank you also to Jacqueline Young, Tareth Mitch, and Albert Tang at Hachette/GCP, and all the others working behind the scenes in production and design and sales and marketing to get my book out to the world. Thank you to my UK co-agents, especially Jemma McDonagh and the entire team at The Marsh Agency. Thank you to my UK publisher, Penguin Random House UK, and the entire team at Ebury Spotlight. Abigail Le Marquand-Brown, thank you for being my UK editor and believing in my story from the jump.

Thank you to all the publicity and marketing experts helping to get this story out to the world: Joseph Papa, Jimmy Franco, Tiffany Porcelli, Alli Rosenthal, Lauren Sum, Patsy O'Neill, Natalia Goncalves, and Amanda Archer.

A special shout-out to Beth Doane, my friend who started me on this journey and encouraged me to share my story.

To my fellow members of the Hugh M. Hefner board, Michael Whelan and Amanda Warren, thank you for being early readers and understanding how important it was for me to speak my truth.

Thank you to the mansion regulars who made my time there more enjoyable: Barbara, Doc, Caela, Ray, Rishiel, Melissa T., Jimmie, Sheila, Carlena, Kea, and the rest of the crew.

I want to thank the many friends who have supported me in this process: Erin E., Shannon, Krystal, Brandon, Melissa S., Amanda V., Carly, Debbie, Erika, Erin F., and Pumehana.

Thank you to all my Hawaii friends who are helping me create a new home. Thank you to all my British friends who help me remember my old home. Thank you to all my California friends who always welcome me home.

My healing journey was also a physical journey, so I'd like to thank the many health pioneers who helped me heal from the mansion: Dr. Ghalili, Dr. Amen, Dr. Horowitz, Dr. Rahbar, Dr. Lehman, and Dr. Shaw.

Thank you to Greg, who first taught me about love. I miss you.

For Lady and Charlie, who taught me about unconditional love. I am so grateful for the companionship, loyalty, and cuteness you've brought into my life. I love you forever.

For my family: Jaydee, Keneisha, Nikki, Melanie, and the rest of my family in England. I love you and thank you for supporting me telling the story of our family as I remember it.

I want to express my heartfelt gratitude to my mother, Lee, my absolute rock and number-one supporter. Your presence in my life is a source of immeasurable joy. Your British humor, quick wit, caring heart, and timeless beauty never fail to amaze me. Your unwavering strength and resilience have been a guiding light. You've tirelessly supported me and consistently strived for my best interests. You immigrated to a new country and faced the loss of a husband, yet your determination to provide the best for your daughters never wavered. I hold an endless love for you, and I am eternally thankful for your constant presence in my life and don't know what I'd ever do without you. I love you.

And finally, for my dad. I know you are proud of me and the best parts of me come from you. Your music plays on in my heart forever.

ABOUT THE AUTHOR

Crystal Hefner is a world-renowned model, advocate, and entrepreneur. A former *Playboy* Playmate, she now works to bring awareness to issues she is passionate about, speaking out on social media to her 10 million followers about body image, objectification, and beauty standards in the media